KILL HITLER

Smuggled out of Berlin, as a three-year-old, Tom Glaser's family settled in Berkhamsted, where he was educated. The horrors of what might have been his fate were always on his mind.

Throughout his career as radio / TV presenter, concurrent with a fashion business, leisure and property development, he always wanted to write about the evils of Nazi Germany.

Now, aged 80, he has realised his ambition and produced three disconnected novels, collectively titled *'Trilogy on World War Two'*. The last of these is *'Kill Hitler'*, preceded by *'A Lowry to Die For'* and *'Eva's War'*.

KILL HITLER

Tom Glaser

KILL HITLER

Olympia Publishers
London

www.olympiapublishers.com
OLYMPIA PAPERBACK EDITION

A CIP catalogue record for this title is
available from the British Library.

ISBN: 978-1-84897-318 3

(Olympia Publishers is part of Ashwell Publishing Ltd)

Apart from Adolf Hitler and Sir Winston Churchill, all the characters in this
book are fictitious and any connection to known persons is coincidental.

First Published in 2013

Olympia Publishers
60 Cannon Street
London
EC4N 6NP

Printed in Great Britain

I dedicate this novel to my parents, Ilse and Arthur Glaser, who had the foresight and courage to leave their home, business and friends in Berlin in 1936 to seek a new life in the United Kingdom.

Acknowledgements

I writer wish to thank the RAF Museum, Hendon for invaluable information on the History and active fighting performance of both Spitfires and Lancasters. These planes on show gave me the inspiration to write about the courage and dedication of those who flew them.

The archives of Elstree Aeorodrome, which recorded the early days of flying, from its predecessor, Aldenham Aerodrome, from which the fragile planes of the day made their maiden flights at very great risk.

The Wagner Festspielhaus at Bayreuth, whose staff were helpful in describing important details about the running of this magnificent venue, for which seats can only be booked 10 years in advance.

The planning authority at Bordeaux regarding the former submarine base at Bacalon, Bassin-a-Flot.

The building still stands today and is now used as a gigantic exhibition centre, showing films and playing concerts. Whilst it is regarded a monument to the horrors of Nazi war-time occupation, the expense and difficulty of demolishing this vast building with six-metre walls is partly responsible for its continued presence. There are plans to create housing around the site at a future date.

Chapter One

I suppose that my story has to begin in Berlin, 1936 – the year of the German Olympiad. Political activity is overwhelming. There's a funny little fellow named Adolf Hitler, who screams and shouts at us on a daily basis. Newspapers, newsreels, posters, there's no getting away from him. People seem to like him, but I think he's funny. I can't believe a word he shouts. I get the distinct impression he doesn't much care for us Jews. I don't understand why that should be. We're all Germans paying our taxes, so why worry? I certainly don't. At age 17, my interests are more sport and women, so I tell my parents, "If he keeps out of my way, I'll keep out of his." Yes, life is good for me. I don't know why my parents should be so worried. They talk about packing up and leaving the country. But how can they? Our roots are firmly imbedded in Berlin.

My Dad has a nice little fashion business, which strangely he named after me. 'Peter Wolf & Co'. I suppose to encourage me to join him in a few years' time when I've left school. He works really hard; gets in at eight and stays all day till late. I'll change all that. I mean, why should the boss have to be there so early? It's anti-social.

I love my sport. I play for my school first football team. I'm tall and use my head well, so I play centre forward and in all modesty I can say I'm the best the school has. I usually score a goal or two and was appointed captain of the team.

I'm very proud of my girlfriend; she goes to the same school. She's beautiful, so natural, and we get on really well in and out of bed. She's not Jewish, but so what. My parents are very laid back about religion. You wouldn't even know that we were a Jewish family at all, except that on Yom Kippur, Mutti puts a notice on the door that says 'Kitchen closed for the day. No entry'. That doesn't stop me from going in and having a discreet nibble. Funny thing – I bumped into Vati last year, doing the same. So we don't take all that stuff too seriously.

I'm quite fortunate to be bilingual. English is my mother language, so I'm top of the class in that subject and the teacher gets worried when she makes a mistake since I pick it up at once. Mother comes from Manchester and she married my German father who is a Berliner. I speak both languages with equal fluency.

I was a bit upset the other day. The football team was posted on the notice board for the next match and my name wasn't there. I couldn't believe my eyes. Old Muller was playing centre – he's useless – and I wasn't in the team at all. God! I scored the winning goal in the last match and was quite a star. Surely I couldn't be dropped after that. I went to see 'Schultzy', such a nice guy, to ask if it was a mistake. "No, no," he said apologetically. "We just want to give Muller a chance, see how he does." He didn't do well and the team lost 2-0. I felt sure I'd be back for the next match. But no, it was Muller again. And again he failed to score. I'm laid back, I know, but interfering with my football is serious. If it happened again I would consider going to the Head some time. But I never did. Nor did I ever play for the school again. Instead, I took my limited talents to the tennis court. I played with my beautiful girlfriend, Tania. And, boy, is she good. Initially she beat me, but then I got better. I took her out one night after a game. I wanted to make love and she wanted to talk. We chose a quiet restaurant for the latter and sadly, the former never happened. She looked lovely as ever that night. The engaging smile, the blonde hair, the blue eyes. She was the best looker in the whole world and I had her all to myself. I knew I was a lucky boy – but evidently not today. She looked serious and her eyes were downcast.

"What's wrong?" said I with as much cheer as I could muster. I could tell she was holding back on me. I held her hand. I could see she had something difficult to tell me.

"Mutti and Vati think we're getting too serious and should spend more time on our studies and less time with each other," she finally came out with it. "Please understand Peter, it's not me." She withdrew her hand from mine and I knew there would be no sex that night. That I could live with, but losing her was another matter.

"I thought you loved me," I appealed. She assured me that she did and suggested that once the holidays started, we would be back together again.

It was only by accident that I caught up with one of Hitler's speeches. Its content was quite conclusive. Suddenly I understood why I was out of the team; even why Tania's parents wished to protect their daughter from the evil clutches of the 'Jewish demon'. I had got the message the hard way. Thank you, Mr Hitler.

Plans were made one evening; I was not consulted. Max and Judy Wolf had seen enough footage to make the decision without my input. As the world watched the Olympics, the Wolf family made its way to Hamburg, whence by *Queen Mary* to England.

Chapter Two

My parents bought a four-bedroom house in a sleepy country town called Berkhamsted, about 25 miles from London. They paid £780 for it, which seemed a lot of money. The one acre plot it stood in was a novelty for me, but I soon got bored with it. They used bedrooms three and four as head offices to restart their business. In Berlin they worked hard. Here it was a slog from dawn till dusk. My father would pack two large suitcases with garments made by outworkers, take the train to affluent towns like Oxford and return with them empty late at night. Exhausted but elated. They wanted me to help so badly. I wish now that I hadn't turned a deaf ear to their appeals. Instead I would take a steam train to Euston and walk the streets of London. I am embarrassed to record the reason. It was to find a girl like Tania.

I was desperately unhappy without her. I walked up Oxford Street, down Regent Street, stopping off at the big stores like Peter Robinson and Dickens & Jones, and wandering aimlessly around them. I saw a lot of pretty girls, but was too shy to speak to any. On one occasion I plucked up the courage to ask a girl in the street if she could direct me to Bond Street. She gave me a funny look and said she didn't know it. I decided to write another letter to Tania, begging her to come to England for a short stay. No doubt it would remain unanswered like the rest.

After a tedious train journey, I decided to walk home the long way round via 'Buck's Meadow', the communal Berkhamsted sports ground. It was rough, but at either end there stood a shabby, neglected goalpost. A group of players was kicking a ball around. I hadn't been near a soccer pitch for months. I longed to join in. I stood and watched them for a while, even applauded some good shots, hoping to get involved. One of the players rested on the touchline to change boots, close to where I was standing. "Nice game," I said trying to start a conversation.

"Bit of practice before the big one," he replied.

"Oh, what's that?"

"The final of our league this Saturday. You play?"

"I do."

"Well come down this time tomorrow. We'll have a kickabout."

"Thanks, I'd like that a lot. I'm Peter Wolf." We shook hands.

"Hi Peter, I'm Bill Rogers."

He pointed to his shock of ginger hair. "Most people call me Ginger."

"Ginger Rogers, where have I heard that name before?"

"I'm still waiting for my first dance with Fred Astaire."

We both laughed. It was the start of a beautiful friendship. As we parted, he waved, "See you here tomorrow then Peter."

"I look forward to it."

Suddenly life without Tania seemed bearable.

It was great to get my gear out of storage. I was excited. I hadn't played since school. Ginger greeted me warmly like the good friend he was to become and introduced me to the other players.

We passed the ball around, tackled and shot at goal. Ginger was a right winger and I moved naturally into my familiar spot at centre forward. There was some rapport between Ginger and me, even on the pitch.

Within the first ten minutes, Ginger came over to me and patted me on the back.

"My God, mate, you're good. Bloody good. How can we book you?"

"Small fee, anytime," I joked. "This ground is terrible, though. Can't we do anything about it?"

17

"Belongs to the council. Never got the money to do anything."

"Can't we do it ourselves?"

I already regarded myself as one of the team.

We stood on the pitch trying to lick the ground into shape. There were bald patches of hard earth, surrounded by clusters of overgrown earth. I trimmed one of them by hand. Worse, there were potholes that could be lethal.

My parents' house had been bought complete with a full kit of gardening equipment.

"I can bring a load of tools with me that will make a big difference," I offered.

The boys cheered and offered to join in the next day and bring tools as well. We played on a little longer and suffered an injury to confirm it was a dangerous playground. Chris Holland, who was marking me at centre, had a nasty fall. He limped off the pitch with a twisted ankle.

"That's me out for Saturday. Sorry mate," he said to Ginger. "This ground's a bloody death-trap."

"We'll clean it up tomorrow. Promise. Give it an ice pack meanwhile."

It was no surprise when Ginger turned to me and out of earshot made the offer.

"You will play for us on Saturday, won't you?"

"Very happy to."

It was obvious that I was streets ahead of Chris Holland. I had beaten him in every tackle.

"Our team is called 'Berks' of Berkhamsted." He added, "Berks by name, but not by nature." We laughed. "Anyway not now that you're playing for us."

"I look forward to it. I'll always do my best."

"Great. Well, the final of the league on Saturday is against a team called Chesham Bois. The prize is that the winning team gets to play a charity match against Tottenham Hotspur on their ground."

"Wow. That's exciting. Up with the big boys."

"Peter, you've been delivered to us at the perfect time."

Suddenly my life was looking good again, even without Tania.

Chapter Three

Bucks Meadow's facelift had transformed it to something closely resembling a football pitch. The team had rallied and turned up in force the next day, complete with multi-purpose garden equipment to do the job. Jack Harris, the resident goalie, had excelled in procuring the use of a tractor, which was trundling up and down the pitch levelling and clearing as it went. Goodness only knows from where, Ginger had found a machine to whiten the lines, so that, hopefully, there would be fewer disputes over penalties. My contribution was to paint the goalposts. By Saturday afternoon, we had a pitch that could do reasonable justice to a local League Final. There was the added attraction of a referee and two line judges. There must have been one hundred spectators, standing behind an improvised rope that allowed the linesman clear access.

My parents had turned up, together with two neighbours who loved to watch a good game. Even the *Gazette* put in an appearance with reporter and photographer to get a good story. The prize was newsworthy – a team of amateurs against the mighty pros of Tottenham Hotspurs.

It was a close match. An angled shot left the goalie stranded. I had scored the winning goal at 2-1.

Ginger seemed to think I was the match winner. He embraced me. "What a find. Best day's work I ever did." He patted me on the back.

"I couldn't have done it without your passes!"

"I hereby offer you life membership."

"I'll only stay as long as you do."

A life-long friendship had been forged.

Chapter Four

The King's Arms was the best, if not the only hotel in Berkhamsted that held a regular Saturday night dinner dance. A classy black-tie affair with a 3-course meal and a six-piece band for five shillings.

The bar needed to be well-stocked, since the 'Berks' had much to celebrate. Some arrived with girl friends. Others, myself included, were hoping to make an acquisition.

"Here's the champ," Ginger called out to me as I arrived. He had a place reserved at his table. He introduced me to his very attractive girl friend, called Suzy. She was talking to her flatmate, as I discovered later, wearing a low-cut dress and a 'Veronica Lake' peroxide hair-do. Her name was 'Bunny'. I think she had been especially lined up for me. Shame, she wasn't my type at all. Her bosom was so well upholstered, that it left little to the imagination. She seemed to be unescorted and I noticed her watching me as I spoke. I must say, I was more interested in Suzy, who reminded me of Tania. While the girls were talking, I said to Ginger:

"Your Suzy's gorgeous."

"You can look," he joked, "but no way touch."

I had the good fortune to have Suzy sitting on one side of me and Bunny the other. It was not easy talking to both, with one ear on the music as well, trying to pick up all the hits of the day. Between toad-in-the-hole and trifle, I was pulled from my chair by Bunny onto the dance floor where she did her professional dance routine. Not an experience I would like to repeat. All eyes were on her as she flaunted herself around at my expense. The 'Berks' cheered wildly at the spectacle and Bunny responded by lifting her red 'Carmen' dress well above her knees. I didn't mind being the centre of attraction on the football field – but on the dance floor, definitely not. Mercifully the band took a break, so that she was able to tease her fans with a conclusive twirl, followed by an over-generous bow that almost released her voluptuous breasts. More to the delight of the applauding 'Berks' than her non-executive partner.

After that, Bunny excused herself for a visit to the toilet, while I withdrew to the bar with Ginger and Suzy.

I told them about Tania and how devastated I had been that she had been obliged to stop seeing me.

"Now you've made such a hit with Bunny, you won't miss her so much."

"Heaven forbid. Too much of a man-eater for me."

"Yeah. She'll gobble you up for breakfast."

"We'll drink to that shall we?"

We ordered beers and whisky chasers. Consumed them and ordered more of the same. I boasted I had never been drunk.

"Not till tonight anyway." Ginger found that funny.

"Look, I've had a few. I can still walk a straight line," I demonstrated.

"No one has ever walked a straighter line, but beware the evening's not over yet."

We bought more drinks to take back to the table. I was pleased to see 'Bunny' on the floor with Rick Lewis, one of the full backs. She waved to me with a flourish as she swept by, doing one of her fancy turns. Rather him than me, I thought. But after the dance she came back to the table, sat on my knee and planted a full-on ruby red kiss on my lips. The boys applauded. Flirtatiously, she said:

"Sorry I was unfaithful to you, darling. You were away too long."

Ginger shouted out for all to hear, "You're gonna score again tonight."

21

Ricky came over to claim another dance. As she rose from my knee, she planted another steamy kiss on my lips. "Wait for me, sweetheart, won't be long."

More cheers from the boys. I emptied the glass in front of me and began to feel the effect. I wasn't used to heavy drinking.

Ginger remarked I had made a conquest and Suzy added to my consternation by telling me what a lovely girl she was: 'without a bad bone in her body'.

"She's my flat-mate, you know. We have a great time together."

We went to the bar to escape the vision of her dancing. The 'straight line' I boasted about earlier, was no longer achievable. Ginger supported me back to the table.

"No more booze for you tonight, I think," he said, putting a kindly arm around my shoulder.

The MC invited everyone on the floor for 'the last waltz'. Rick came over to claim his prize. Bunny was not going to leave me.

"I have to stay with my baby for this one," she said and pulled me back onto the floor.

It was a slow waltz, thank God. I couldn't have stayed upright for anything more. She was quite happy to stay close, taking small steps. I was not so drunk that I couldn't feel her leg between mine and an arm that massaged my neck. She must have felt a twinge, because she said, "Later, my darling."

She kissed me again, deeply, passionately, and held my hand in hers when all stood straight for the National Anthem. I can't remember too much about what happened next, only that I was in a taxi with Ginger, Suzy and Bunny. I felt a hand stroke my inner thighs and an excited exclamation from Bunny, "Wow. Feels good."

Although I had not been invited officially, I understood that we were heading for the flat shared by Suzy and Bunny. Ginger, obviously, knew his way around. It was a ground floor 2 bedroom apartment in Charles Street. We had more drinks and Suzy played the gramophone with her favourite Ella Fitzgerald songs. Bunny disappeared to the toilet for what seemed an eternity. Finally she emerged, with a new face of make-up, lips even redder than before. She set about me, making it clear that there could only be one outcome to the evening.

"I would like to lie down now, my sweetheart," she breathed softly in my ear before kissing me passionately on the mouth. She was not going to take 'no' for an answer. She took my hand and led me to her bedroom. The softness of a manicured hand inside my pants took me to the point of no return. In a flash, the dress that had contained her curvaceous body was pulled over her head. Knickers and brassiere were to follow quickly. There was enough light for me to observe that she had a beautiful figure. I could not help noticing that her pubic hair did not correspond to the peroxide 'Veronica Lake' that she had been tossing about all evening. Although mostly shaved, the stubble was black. Fully nude, she wiggled her body seductively before me, to increase my appetite even further; then she lay beside me, her hands running amok over all my sensitive areas. Her searching tongue seemed to have a life of its own. She took my hand and placed it on her shaven crotch. She groaned in appreciation as my fingers explored the region. She finally knew that her prey had succumbed. I was made aware that more activity on my part was required. I kissed her nipples each in turn, before working my tongue over her abdomen. She said it tickled her and giggled. Maybe at my efforts to play the grand lover. But her groaning intensified as she opened her legs. At this point she whispered in my ear in a very sexy voice:

"Don't worry, sweetheart. I'm wearing a cap."

Now I understood her prolonged visit to the toilet earlier. I closed my eyes and thought of Tania.

Chapter Five

"Honestly, Suzy, it's safe as houses."

"Well, if you want to see me worry day and night, you'll go through with it."

"You'd get used to it – I promise you. Safer than crossing the road these days."

"I'm begging you not to do it."

"But this is my chosen career. I can't give it up. I love you with all my heart, darling Suzy, but please say it's OK. I beg you."

I was cracking my hard-boiled egg over breakfast next morning, when I caught the tail end of their conversation. I had left Bunny in bed, exhausted from her nocturnal activity. I must say I felt a bit shaky myself with a bad headache, but had to enquire of my friend what this hotly contested career might be.

"It's very simple Peter," he started to explain, "I'm learning to fly; I love it so much, I want to join the Air Force. Get a commission, make a career of it. I'd be able to make a decent pile and do something I enjoy."

Suzy was out of earshot, cooking toast in the kitchen. I lowered my voice to a whisper. "How dangerous is it?"

Ginger looked around uncomfortably to make sure Suzy was still in the kitchen.

"It's bloody dangerous, I can tell you, suicidal in fact. But by God it's exciting. The moment the wheels leave the ground, you're in another world. I can't describe the feeling. You have to do it to know it."

"So where's the danger, then?" I enquired with fascination.

Before he could reply, Suzy came into the room with a generous plateful of toast, butter and marmalade.

"Bunny's going to stay in bed all day," she declared to the boys. "What on earth did you do to her Peter? I just brought her some tea, she drank it and said goodnight, see you in the morning. Shame. It's such a lovely day."

We ate her toast, not daring to mention the dreaded career.

My head was throbbing. I suggested a walk to clear my brain.

"You go with Ginger," she said, "while I do the flat, then I've got some lines to learn, so don't be in a hurry to come back."

A perfect opportunity to have an unencumbered chat with him about his problem. I asked her what the play was. Casually she informed me that she was doing Ophelia.

"What a role," I said "You will make sure I have a ticket. You as Ophelia, that's something I have to see. I love *Hamlet* anyway."

Walking briskly, we headed for the common. On the way, a few cracks about my sexual prowess, but it wasn't long before the subject of Ginger's flying career cropped up again. I was intrigued by the combination of danger and excitement.

"So where do you do your flying?" I broached the subject carefully. I got a lengthy explanation.

"Have you heard of Aldenham?" he asked. I hadn't. He told me all about it. It's a mansion with acres and acres of surrounding land. Lord Aldenham's son spent vast amounts of cash converting it to a country club, complete with tennis and squash courts, golf courses and polo pitches. It's become a fashionable playground for the wealthy socialites. Then Captain Watkins came up with the idea of introducing an airstrip on a near zero budget. Flying was the new thing, and he was quick to see the commercial possibilities.

"Like what?" I interrupted him.

"Tons of stuff. There's joyriding at five shillings a time, trailing advertising banners, instruction and above all getting from A to B. Flying's the newest thing; the biggest invention of the thirties."

"Makes sense," I agreed.

"Anyway I got to know the captain and he trained me to become his assistant. Honestly, it's a whole new world. I love flying now. Safe as houses – once you're airborne."

"So what's Suzy so worried about then?"

"Well… Captain Watkins hasn't got the money together yet to do the runway. The strip is grim. Full of potholes, cracks and crevices, long grass and stones. The little wheels of the plane just can't handle the rough ground. That's the most frightening part of it."

"Why in God's name doesn't he fix it? Sounds horrendous."

"Simple. He hasn't got the money… yet. He will have soon."

"Soon might be too late."

"Give the guy a chance. First he bought a DH90 Dragonfly. He taught me to fly it and from then on we started making a bit of money. The demand was so great that we had to buy a second one. When that's paid for, we do the runway. Rome wasn't built in a day. We'll do it all slowly… slowly."

"It sounds precarious to put it mildly."

"Once you take off, there's another little hazard you have to negotiate; high tension cables and pylons across the runway. It's scary, it really is."

I interrupted, "It sounds horrific. You must be just a little mad to do it."

He continued, "I probably am, but I tell you, once you have survived the take-off, dodged the cables and you're airborne, you experience the most fantastic exhilaration I've ever known. Gliding between the clouds, seeing the countryside below – Oh boy, it's another world, magnificent. I would challenge anyone to take the risk – the rewards are so great."

Possibly because my head was clearing, possibly because I wanted to cement the bond between Ginger and myself, I made the most stupid remark of my life. "I'd like to give it a shot." I actually said those words, although my brain was rejecting them the moment they were spoken.

Chapter Six

I couldn't eat my breakfast on the day. The night before, sleep was anything but sound. I sort of hoped that Ginger might forget to come. But no, on the dot of 9.00 a.m., the doorbell rang and there he was in fur-lined flying jacket and boots.

"Hi partner," he greeted me, obviously without a care in the world.

"Come and look at my new gillopy. Cost a fortune... £25... crazy the prices dealers dream up these days."

I left the house-door ajar to look over his purchase. It was a bright red 2-seater MG.

"Chose the colour to match my hair," he giggled.

I managed a wry smile. Laughing was not on my agenda that day. I voiced my trepidations.

"D'you think I should do it?" I asked tentatively.

"'Course you bloody should. It's a piece of cake. You'll be right as rain. Safe as houses."

He always spoke in clichés, but three in one sentence was a bit much even for him.

"With me in the driving seat, you can't go wrong. Just got my wings. Passed with flying colours."

Hearing that he was to be my pilot and instructor made me feel a whole lot worse. I had got myself into this mess and now I had to go through with it or lose face.

The drive to Aldenham took fifty minutes of hell. The country roads were congested and so, it seems, were my vocal chords, since I uttered not one word. Ginger spoke in monologues about the wonderful opportunities that would open up to him, now he had his licence.

"Suzy's accepted that this will be my career, so everyone's happy."

Recalling her fierce opposition, I wondered whether this might be wishful thinking on his part.

"Here we are," he said pointlessly, since there was a gigantic circle at the centre of the site with ten feet high letters proclaiming that this was in fact ALDENHAM. The sight of little planes dotted around the apron sent a shiver down my spine. How could these fragile little machines ever get airborne? The answer was imminent. A Gloster Gladiator bi-plane was revving its engine, ready for take-off. The pilot waved to Ginger as he passed us by. Ginger shouted over the noise, "Have a good flight, Buddy." The little plane hobbled over the rough ground, then gathered speed. The wings dipped one way, then the other as it struck loose stones on the runway. I breathed a sigh of relief when take-off happened without incident. I heard Ginger mutter, "Nice take-off, Buddy," then to me, "watch him bank now and sharply, to miss the cables. There he goes."

"Why don't you get together and do something about all these hazards?" I asked timidly.

"Because the runway's 750 yards long and Captain Watkins doesn't have the money right now. I'm sure he will get it done soon."

I mumbled, "Yes after the first crash, I'm sure he will. Just hope it's not me."

"Well, there's more to it than that," he replied,

"You see, because of the overhead cables, we can only get planning permission three months at a time. So it could be…"

"…if there's a crash in the meantime," I interrupted…

"…that at some point we may have to close the aerodrome. And that's why the Captain won't spend until he knows we can continue to operate," concluded Ginger.

"That's good to hear," I said with a tinge of sarcasm.

Ginger parked the MG as near to the offices as he could get, and went in. He told me to book take-off in thirty minutes' time. Then we walked.

"There she goes," said Ginger after five minutes, "the finest little plane you could ever wish to fly in."

I looked it up and down with fear in my eyes.

'A monster in repose,' I thought to myself. I had to admit it had good-looking lines. Silver and green, two-tone, a twin-engined bi-plane, I was told, called the DH90 Dragonfly.

"Taught me alright and so it will you," were his last words as we clambered aboard. Ginger showed me how to 'strap up', which I did as well as my trembling hands would allow. A few words about the controls and how they could be passed from pilot to passenger. 'Not much chance of that happening,' I thought and the monster suddenly came to life. The smell of fumes assailed me through the open cockpit window as the engine was coaxed into full throttle.

Ginger checked that all the instruments and controls were functioning correctly. Then slowly, he edged the plane forward to the edge of the runway. He closed the cockpit windows and took the Dragonfly to full power. Moving at speed down the bumpy runway was quite the most frightening part of the flight. But it was only for a few seconds and when we were airborne, there was a strange feeling of relief that maybe the worst bit of the flight had been overcome. Then came a sharp bank to remind me of the hidden danger of the cables. I was strangely calm as the plane headed upwards into the sky. I ventured a look out of the window. It was as though we were stationary and the ground below was moving away from under us. I thought it safer to look ahead.

Ginger seemed to enjoy my discomfort. He manoeuvred the little craft, banking steeply, first left then right. It seemed to me that our position was near to right-angular, defying the laws of gravity. I held tightly to my straps, praying that they would take my weight if the plane rolled over. Ginger guided his plane elegantly from cloud to blue sky and back to cloud again. Whilst in the process, he turned and shouted to me:

"You OK?" and seeing I was anything but, he added, "Great isn't it?"

Then, frighteningly, he took the plane into a steep dive that must have thrown us what seemed a few thousand feet earthwards. I held onto my straps for grim life. I may even have screamed. My stomach churned over and over; my heart missed several beats. Ginger took the time to glance at me to gauge my reaction. Whatever he saw, he must have taken pity on me, since he pulled out of the dive at a point when it seemed to me that collision with the world below was inevitable.

"That was fun," he shouted.

I nodded, praying this party piece might be the end of his showmanship.

"Time for you to have a go," he shouted.

He switched control to the passenger side and told me what to do. I was relieved to be holding a steady course. Slowly I got the feel of the little plane's agility and the guidance required to move it around.

I moved the joystick very gently and got a slight bank leftwards; then straightened and to the right. I followed the procedure several times. I felt strangely akin to the aircraft as it answered commands, much more comfortable as pilot than passenger.

As we shimmered through the sky, dodging clouds, playing hide and seek with the sun, I was actually beginning to relax, even enjoy the experience.

"You're doing well," Ginger shouted at me. "Ready to land?"

I thought he was being serious, "What me?"

I wouldn't have put it past him.

"Next time," he shouted.

He took control back and gently we glided earthwards. As the wheels made contact with the ground, there was a sharp bump followed by three bounces as we came to a grinding halt.

"Phew. That was something of a nightmare," I exclaimed when the engine was switched off. "If you only knew how close I was to calling the whole thing off..."

He took over, "...and now you're glad you didn't."

I couldn't believe I was saying it: "So when do we fly again?"

Chapter Seven

I took sunglasses from the breast pocket of my flying suit. I had broken through the cloud barrier and was facing an unprotected sun.

It was deep azure blue around me. At 1500 feet I skimmed over the white blanket below and rejoiced in the serenity of my solo flight. But for purring engine, I might have been gliding. Total solitude. Just me and the machine, moving at my whim.

I had to smile when I recalled the sheer terror of my first flight. Now I was confident in the machine and my ability to fly it. Ginger had been unkind to me on that first flight. There had been no need to go into a sharp dive. But I liked him all the more for his perseverance. He had bullied me mercilessly into flying on a daily basis. Then came my first solo flight. Terror of a different kind. No-one to turn to. Finally the test to acquire my licence. The elation of becoming a qualified Class 1 pilot. I couldn't have done it without Ginger's help. I owed him a debt of gratitude. I wasn't yet his equal in the air, but it pleased me that on the football pitch I had the edge. We did things together on a daily basis. I liked it that way and did all I could to cement our 'brotherhood'. In his inevitably clichéd dialogue, he said:

"We're joined at the hip, like two peas in a pod."

The big football match with Tottenham Hotspur was finally to be played on Saturday. 'Berks' were fully trained and ready. The match had been twice postponed, due to Tottenham's commitments. Playing a charity match with an unknown amateur league team came very low on their list of priorities. I had invited Tania to come over from Berlin for the match, but she declined.

'There is so much unrest here,' she wrote, 'I think it would be unwise to make such a long journey. I may not be able to get back.' She went on to explain that the Poles were being very aggressive on their frontier with Germany. In a skirmish they had killed two German soldiers and captured three more. The Führer said there would be serious repercussions for this aggression.

'It could lead to war,' Mutti and Vati warned her. 'Poland has an agreement that England would protect her, if attacked and I could be left away from home if there was a war.' I was a little upset that she allowed her head to rule her heart, but why should I? She'd done it before and it should not have come as a surprise. It cleared my conscience and I felt free to continue my relationship with Bunny: when required.

I was flying in a northwesterly direction, enjoying the sunshine. My dials told me it was time to turn for home. I banked sharply, descended below the clouds and after a while recognised the landmarks that led me to the aerodrome. Ginger watched my safe but bumpy landing and I taxied the plane over rough ground to where he was standing.

"Nice touchdown," he said. "Give it ten years; you'll be as good as me."

"Cheeky Bastard," I replied. "I'll give you a lesson on the football pitch any time you want."

From then on, our conversation and thoughts were only on the forthcoming match.

Ginger and I had been to White Hart Lane to get a feel for the place. The home team were impressive.

"They're bloody good," I voiced my opinion, "but they can't do anything we can't."

I was waiting for him to come up with some comment on the lines of 'David and Goliath'. I wasn't far wrong.

"St George killed the dragon," he said profoundly, "and we will do likewise."

Famous last words, I thought. The Spurs attack was relentless. At 2-1 down we were awarded a penalty.

Ginger took the ball and placed it carefully on the spot, taking time to clean and check his boots before taking the vital kick which would have given us an historic draw. The team and supporters alike collectively held its breath. The stadium was silent. Ginger took six confident strides and aimed right-footed for the left corner. The goalie, anticipating the shot with the reflexes of a cat, made a spectacular one-handed save.

After the match, Ginger sat on a bench in the changing room, devastated by his missed opportunity. I put my arm around his shoulder and consoled him.

"Don't worry, mate. We played a great game and nearly got a result. Too bad the goalie was left-handed." Then I had to score a point.

"Next time there's a penalty – do us all a favour and let me take it."

He pushed me away and smiled. "The next time there's a big kick, it'll be up your arse."

That's the way our relationship was these days. Plenty of cut and thrust over an underlying bond of deep friendship and respect.

After we had showered, Bill Nicholson, the Spurs captain, cornered Ginger and me.

"Well played, lads. I'd like to have a private chat with you two, if you can spare a minute."

Ginger and I exchanged quizzical glances. We agreed to meet him in the bar in ten minutes.

"So what's all that about?" Ginger exclaimed. "Maybe he wants to discuss your missed penalty," I suggested.

We bought two pints and sat at a table as far away from the noise of the bar as possible. Presently Mr Nicholson arrived with a tall, athletic looking lady, whom he introduced as the club secretary, Helen Judd. This led us to believe that some sort of a business discussion was to follow. Mr Nicholson was very complimentary.

"A fantastic little team you have. 2-1 that could, should, have been 2-2 is a brilliant result for you."

Ginger blushed at the obvious reference to his missed penalty, but said nothing, waiting to hear what Mr Nicholson had in mind.

"I'm managing the team and the target is Division 1," he continued. We were all aware that Tottenham had slipped to the second division and was only lying seventh. Not in danger of relegation, but not in contention for promotion.

"The Board of Directors has engaged me as manager and given me the task to take the club back to its rightful position at the top of the first division. We have to win it. No less than that."

Ginger and I looked at one another in delight, since the object of the meeting had become self-explanatory. We didn't say a word and left Mr Nicholson to elaborate.

"I was impressed with the spirit of your team," he continued, "and to my mind, you two were its leading players."

We smiled at the compliment. Ginger replied, "Thanks Mr Nicholson, we try our best…"

"And your best looks pretty good to me," he interjected before Ginger had a chance to say any more.

"I'll come to the point. Would you be interested in becoming professional players?"

Things couldn't get much better than being asked that question by the manager of one of the leading clubs in the land. We couldn't wait to assure him in the affirmative. Mr Nicholson told us that the club was introducing an apprentice squad of young talented players, with the intention of grooming them to play for the club's first team.

"You won't be earning a fortune to begin with – five pounds per week – but once in the first team that'll go up to seven. Then there's a win bonus and another if you score. So that's the deal. Fancy it?" We nodded combined approval. Ginger spoke for us both.

"We are honoured and excited by the offer."

I said that I had always been a Tottenham supporter and perhaps one day to play for them, would be beyond my wildest dreams. Ginger couldn't resist the opportunity of getting in on the act.

"The first rung of the ladder and the most exciting it could ever be," he quipped.

"Would you like to take the contract away with you to think it over," Mr Nicholson concluded, "or sign it here and now, in which case, Helen has all the paperwork ready."

There was nothing to think over and we said we were happy to be signed up. "The quicker the better," said Ginger.

"In that case," Mr Nicholson said rising, "I'll leave you with Helen to complete the formalities and I'll be in touch with you shortly to give you training times and matches that you will be expected to attend, even if you're not part of the squad." We shook hands on the deal and said that we were looking forward to working with him and would do our level best to help the club's return to the top of the first division.

As we drove home, we could hardly believe our good fortune. We celebrated that night, the four of us. Suzy was happy about the career change; Bunny appeared excited at the prospect of another night with me.

The Sunday papers were dire. Germany had invaded Poland. Neville Chamberlain issued an ultimatum that if Germany did not cease its hostilities against Poland at once, the United Kingdom would come to her aid. Hitler ignored the threat. At 11.00 a.m. on the 3rd September 1939, Chamberlain told the nation: *'We are now at war with Germany.'*

On that same day, League football was abandoned for the duration.

Chapter Eight

We saluted the Squadron Leader smartly on entering his office.

"Good Morning gentlemen," he said. "Take a pew."

He shuffled some papers and presumably found the ones he was looking for.

"So I see you're professional footballers," he stated, not looking up. Ginger explained our story of 'nearly', and we were promised a place on the RAF team.

"RAF Football Association," he gave us some gratuitous information, "works out of Martlesham Heath station at Woodbridge Suffolk. I'll give the Hon Sec. a ring if you wish."

We thanked him for his consideration.

"Grand," he said with enthusiasm.

Thus reassured, we felt sufficiently relaxed to assess our surroundings. A small plaque on his desk that stated his name and rank confirmed that we were sitting in the office of Squadron Leader Kit Palmer. He was an impressive looking man in his forties, with a beautiful speaking voice. The decorations on his jacket told us that he was one of those brave young men who had taken the fragile warplanes of WW1 into the skies over the battlefields of France. Unkempt whisks of hair protruded from beneath his peaked cap. Whether they were connected with anything on top was not revealed, since he kept it firmly in place.

Through the window of his musty office, we could hear and see the activity of a dozen or so airplanes, preparing to take off on a training flight. I recognised them to be a mix of Gauntlet biplanes and Gloster Gladiators. The office was sparsely furnished, comprising of a few chairs, a shabby settee and two desks. Framed photos of his family and dog stood beside one of himself, sitting in the cockpit of a WW1 Lysander. A spent packet of Players cigarettes lay in the large ashtray, so full of 'fag-ends', that it was clear that he had been the occupant for some time. He took a new packet of Kensitas from his pocket, opened it and offered us contents.

"Thanks, we don't," I declined for both of us.

"Shocking habit," he declared, lighting up with relish and showing his nicotine-stained fingers in the process. "My wife complains I come home smelling like a polecat."

We laughed politely. Outside, one of the small planes was revving up noisily, which killed any conversation as it taxied for take-off. He puffed away contentedly, inhaling deeply. Ginger and I exchanged glances beginning to wonder why we had been summoned for this meeting. We had been singled out from a group of 12 young Pilot Officers who had graduated a crash course at RAF Cranwell. They came with a commission on discharge marked 'ready for action'. Most of what they had taught us, we already knew. As far as flying was concerned, it was a waste of time. We were proud to have joined the ranks of commissioned officers in the Royal Air Force. There was an element of urgency when we sought permission to be posted to the same unit. So it came about that we, Ginger and I, found ourselves together with Number 19 Squadron at Duxford. We were informed that it was lined up to dump the obsolete Gauntlet bi-planes in favour of what was described as 'the latest and greatest fighter aircraft in the history of aviation'. We were excited and eager to hear more about it. We sat in silence as the Squadron Leader puffed away, waiting for the din to subside. Finally he stubbed it out and started to tell us what the meeting was about.

"We are one of the first squadrons to get it," he exclaimed, "and by God we're going to use it! Show Jerry who's master of the sky, if they dare to venture over our island."

His manicured voice sounded almost Churchillian. Dramatically he pulled a picture from the drawer of his desk.

"This, gentlemen, is it. The finest little fighter in the sky." He paused, allowing us time to study the picture. "Grand isn't she? Just grand."

We had to agree it looked a lot more modern than the old planes circulating the runways outside.

"This is the MK 1 Spitfire that's going to win us the war." He pointed to the single propeller, its eight cannons and told us it was powered by Rolls Royce Merlin engine. "It's a great package," he summed up. "All we need are pilots to fly it!"

"Shouldn't be a problem," I interjected.

"You'd think not, but it is. You see this is a more sophisticated plane. It has all sorts of gadgets and new developments. Its manoeuvrability is second to none. It has great speed, better armament and flexibility. Handling it to full advantage has to be learnt. You've seen the German Messerschmitt fighters on the newsreels, – the Spitfire will shoot the shit out of them. If the German bombers come over, they'll be slaughtered by our 'Spits'. The factories are on full-scale production. Beaverbrook hopes to have 150 squadrons equipped with them in a year's time. We have to pray it's time enough to complete the programme."

A further cigarette had to be lit. I took the opportunity to enquire when the first of the Spitfires would be delivered.

"This takes me to my point," he replied. "Delivery will come in about four weeks, which will get us in the air. But here's the good news: In hanger B, we have a proto."

We were excited to hear it.

"Love to have a butchers," Ginger said.

"And so you shall," said the Squadron Leader. "More than a butcher's. I want you two lads to fly her. By day and night on 24 hour call. I want you to learn every move it can make. Its acceleration, its speed and angle of climbing. Its diving capacity. I want you to sleep with it, live with it and think of nothing but how it can fool and outwit our adversaries. And when you know absolutely everything about it there is to know, I want the pair of you to teach the squadron how to fly it."

He paused for more smoking time after his eloquent explanation.

"Why us?" we enquired.

"Why you?" he repeated the question. "Because you two, between you have got close to 8000 flying hours chalked up. I'm fed up to the back teeth with these fucking Johnnies who think they can fly after a few hours at Cranwell."

We were quite shocked to hear his lapse of language – but so beautifully enunciated. I enquired why he was so disillusioned with the new intake.

"We've had six fatalities in the last month. Not one of them by enemy action," he fumed angrily. "Six pilots dead and six planes written off. Just stupid bloody fool mistakes. One of the silly bastards forgot to lower his wheels on landing. That was a new plane gone west. Another went into a dive and forgot how to pull out on time. Fucking idiot," he let rip. "So now, start of a new era – if Jerry allows us the time," he added with an air of foreboding. "I want you two lads to vet, coach and train every new arrival. Not to let them near the controls of any plane, old or new, until you declare them competent to fly it." He paused while lovingly fondling another cigarette before lighting it. He took a drag, which seemed to calm him.

"Do I make myself clear? Not one pilot is to fly in this squadron until you say he can."

We both replied that we understood him perfectly.

He continued, "Time is not on our side. The enemy might attack at any moment, now that France is on the way out, and I want to feel confident that any pilot taking off from this station is able to get the best out of his airplane. Particularly as it's likely to be a Spitfire."

He tapped the first layer of ash into an already full tray. Ginger and I felt it was time for us to speak.

"Sir," said I, "we are truly proud to serve under you in 19 Squadron and you may rely on us to meet your wishes to the best of our ability."

"That's grand," he replied and repeated with emphasis, "really grand."

Ginger asked when we were to start work.

"Now... right now," he semi-shouted. "We've got to get this fucking squadron fit to fight within four weeks. I pray we've got that long."

We made the obvious point that we needed to know all about the Spitfire ourselves, before we could teach others.

"Well let's not waste another moment talking about it. Let's get on with it." To show he meant what he said, he stubbed out a half-smoked cigarette with an air of immediate work to be done. "Let me introduce you to our new toy. You'll see her in the flesh. She's a beauty."

He attempted to rise from his chair to indicate the meeting over, but fell back. He picked up a single crutch from the floor that helped him stay upright. Ginger and I rushed to help him to his feet. We had no idea he had a problem.

"It's OK, I don't need any help," he said proudly. "I've learnt to live on one leg."

That said, he propped himself up onto the crutch and limped at fair speed in the direction of Hangar B. On the way there he told us the story. "The Huns got me the last week of the war. My leg was paralysed, but after six months in hospital, they got me on my feet. Slowly but surely I started to walk again. Within a year I was back at work. Twenty good years I had and then the gangrene got me. Nice options– amputate or die. I thought that death might be better, if only I could find a decent way to do it. My wife wasn't going to let that happen. So now I manage on one leg, just waiting and counting the days for a specially modified Spit that I can fly to lead my squadron to revenge. Fucking Huns," he added for good measure. "It can't come soon enough!"

"And when it does, sir, we'll be right behind you every inch of the way."

We shook hands to confirm our support. With the aid of his crutch, he pushed open the hangar door. We stood looking at the machine in stunned silence. We felt her, touched her, sat in her cockpit and revved up her engine.

"Such elegance," we both said. "Sheer beauty."

"Wait 'till you fly her," said the Squadron Leader. "Just one word to describe her. Grand, just bloody, fucking grand."

Chapter Nine

'The battle of France is over. The battle of Britain is about to begin.'

Thus spoke Winston Churchill, addressing the Commons in sombre mood. The speech was heard on the wireless in the officers' mess at Duxford Station. There were cheers of approval from the assembled pilots. Sitting about, waiting for the enemy to strike, did not suit them.

"If there's going to be a war," they said, "then for Christ's sake, let's get on with it."

They were not to know that their 'Supremo' Air Chief Marshal Hugh Dowding had rejected with a flat refusal, the French appeal for more Spitfire squadrons to halt the German invasion of their country.

Prophetically, he warned, "Run out of Spitfires and we're DEAD." He was known for his dry and economical use of the English language. Never use two words, when one will do.

The pilots knew the onslaught was imminent. They understood that the defence of the nation would rest on their shoulders. They were ready to engage the enemy. Confidence in their ability to shoot the Hun bombers out of the sky was high. Their training had been intense.

Ginger and I had shaped the young pilots into a formidable fighting force. Now there was an appetite to put their skills to the test. Above all else, speed of getting airborne fast was crucial. They had been taught that a delay of only one minute, could lose 2000 feet of altitude; and that could make the difference between success and failure.

"Get the hell up there fast," we instructed day after day, "and swoop down on the bombers, the sun behind you."

Squadron Leader Kit Palmer was overjoyed that his influx of 'rookie' pilots had turned into a fighting force that he was proud to lead.

"You've done a grand job training them," he congratulated us, and with it came promotion to 'Flying Officer'.

"Gives us a bit of extra pocket money," said Ginger. "Now we can really go 'high life'," he smiled.

Saturday 15th August 1940 is a date I will never forget. Warm, hazy, end-of-summer sunshine. The crews were idling away their time, coping with the boredom of a 'phoney war', that seemingly would never ignite. Some were dozing in the sun; others flat out on their bunks. Ginger was playing chess with Douggie Owen, whilst Kit Palmer was hidden behind a double page spread of *The Times*, with clouds of smoke billowing from beneath it. I had always been fascinated by the sonorous tone of his speaking voice, but felt it would be disrespectful to enquire its origins. Today, with very little to do, but talk and relax, I ambled over in his direction to see if I could get into conversation with him.

"Lovely day," was my opening gambit. It wasn't enough for him to put down the paper. "The war doesn't look too good," I tried again. That started him off.

"Always said the so-called 'Treaty of Versailles' was World War 2 in the making – and now we have it."

He put down the paper to register his disgust. We talked a little more of how Hitler had turned the tables on his conquerors with such ease and now we were paying dearly for not standing up to him earlier. He seemed quite ready to chat, so I ventured a leading question.

"Sir, what will you do when it's all over?"

He dwelt on his reply for some seconds. "Nothing much you can do on one leg, is there?"

I suggested politely, inquisitively, "Sir, what with that voice of yours, there's plenty you can do."

43

"Ah yes," he pondered, columns of smoke drifting upwards. "The voice – true enough, that's still there. Good enough to announce trains at a railway station," he joked. We both laughed. "But seriously," he went on, "there's not too many parts going for one-legged actors – particularly an old 'ham' like me."

I gave myself a mental pat on the back. I had broken down the barriers. I had got him onto a subject he enjoyed. Pushing home my advantage, I asked what kind of roles he had played.

He smiled at the memory. "Anything that came up. In Rep it was mainly comedy, but then, believe it or not, I got myself a little known for doing Shakespeare."

I told him I most certainly could believe it. "That voice is capable of anything. When I first heard you speak, sir, I knew you had to be a singer or actor or similar."

He looked away and I thought I could detect a tear running down his cheek. He composed himself.

"Very kind of you to say so. Thank you. Yes, I still have my voice; I can still remember my lines and I can still do Shakespeare as well as any of the big boys. We'll have to see how it goes after the War."

After a slight pause, with total spontaneity, he gave me a gratuitous example of a past role: He didn't speak the familiar lines, he acted them with that resonant, penetrating voice. With eyes flashing and clenched fist, he burst into the speech that was so appropriate to the current mood.

"Once more unto the breach, dear friends, once more.

Or close the wall up with our English dead.

In peace there's nothing so becomes a man as a modest stillness and humility.

But when the blast of War blows in our ears, then imitate the action of the tiger.

Stiffen the sinews, summon up the blood.

Disguise fair nature with hard-favoured rage.

Then lend the eye a terrible aspect."

I stood to applaud. He spoke the lines so perfectly; I was both moved and impressed.

"How long ago did you do Henry V?"

He stated it must have been a good 20 years.

"And you still know it so well?" He seemed flattered at my interest.

"Once I've learnt and played a part – I know it, for life. What chance to play it again – Henry V on one leg? Doesn't quite gel."

I was keen to show off my knowledge. "Richard III was a bit one legged, I seem to remember."

He sighed deeply. "But would they want an old ham like me to play him?"

I could tell how excited he had become to talk about his far-distant theatrical career that I wanted to prolong the dialogue.

"What other roles did you play?"

He looked skywards and I could tell he was searching his memory for some of the important milestones of his career. "Well, there was 'Iago' in Stratford – a great production that ran and ran. 'Laertes' in Hamlet. 'Kent' in King Lear... I could go on all day," he chuckled. "Always the bridesmaid, never the bride." Always on tour. Never made the West End. Summer Rep in every seaside resort you could think of – Felixstowe, Cromer, Skegness, Scarborough. Great days they were, until disaster struck me down. I was in and out of hospital forever and no one seemed to remember me at casting time." A gentle smile turned into a throaty laugh. "No, I tell a lie," he reflected. "One of my mates did remember me. He re-wrote an Agatha Christie play and put 'Poirot' in a wheelchair – just so that I could play him." He burst out laughing. "Imagine Poirot in a wheelchair with one leg. Hilarious. Oh yes, he still got his man."

I laughed with him. I was happy to be reminiscing with him and I detected the signs of friendship coming on.

"I've got a scrapbook at home with all my parts, photos, programmes and so on. Haven't looked at it in years. Maybe now's the time to pick it up again."

I told him I would love to spend time with him and study his scrapbook. "I could listen to your show-biz stories all day."

"That's grand," he said. "We'll do it, grand."

The conversation ended abruptly. The siren sounded. All of a sudden the station came to life. Inert bodies became active. There was a stampede towards the waiting planes. Shouts of: "300-plus crossed the coast. This is it. Let's get amongst them."

The Squadron Leader had to wait for his special motorized trolley to arrive with ground crew. He was frustrated to be left standing, while the first planes were already taking off. He lifted up the phone and screamed into it. Gone was the sweet-tongued Shakespearean actor.

"Where the fucking hell are you? I'm supposed to be the first in the air. Not the fucking last."

"Sorry, sir," a voice came back, "we're on the way."

Thirty seconds later the flat-bottom truck arrived and skidded to a halt. Without further abuse, the Squadron Leader was hoisted aboard and bundled unceremoniously into the cockpit of his specially constructed Spitfire. Take-off was achieved in record time. Even so, he was at least one and a half minutes behind the squadron. It was flying in a V Wing formation and his place should have been at the Apex, directing the squadron and identifying the target. His dependence on others left him feeling inadequate. He had been preaching the vital importance of getting in the air quickly, and now, at first test, when it mattered most, he had let them all down. He gave his Merlin engine a full throttle and climbed steeply in pursuit of his squadron. He switched the inter-com:

"This is Skipper calling. Sorry, I missed the bus on take-off. Ginger, please lead V formation. I'll be tail-end Charlie. Good luck. Over and out."

Moments later Ginger's voice crackled over the airwaves, "Message understood. Willco. Roger and out."

They continued to gain altitude while Ginger moved to the apex of the wing; as he broke through a thick layer of cloud, he made first visual contact of an aerial Armada hovering just beneath cloud cover. Instinctively he took his squadron 1000 feet higher to maximise the dive, the sun behind them. As he roared upwards, then banked, the full extent of the enemy became apparent. His heart missed several beats. The mass of swastikas and black crosses made it difficult to assess numbers. There were Junkers, Heinkels, that he identified at once, flying at staggered heights, escorted by Messerschmitt fighters on a two to one ratio. Swarms of them. This was the supreme moment of action, the moment they had been trained to handle for the last year. He tried to steady his voice and sound relaxed as he broke radio silence:

"Bandits at 3 o'clock. Climbing to attack from above. This is it. Enjoy the party. Over and out."

The wing was right behind him as they peeled off one after the other to attack. Ginger was the first to strike. The Heinkel pilot would hardly have seen him coming out of the sun. He had impetus and surprise. He wouldn't have known about it until the Spitfire's cannons had spoken in anger. Three bursts were enough to dispatch the luckless bomber. A Messerschmitt fighter came to help belatedly, but by then the Spitfire had banked away in search of new prey. Ginger felt elated at his first kill. From out of the corner of his eye, he saw parachutes open and drift earthwards. Just in time, since moments later the doomed plane, its bomb-load intact, ended its flight history with an enormous explosion and spiralled to the ground.

The battle moved westwards as the bombers continued their journey. The Spitfires were diving in and out, shooting at whatever crossed their path. I was determined to make a kill myself; otherwise Ginger's one-upmanship would have been intolerable. I found myself on a near collision course with a bomber. He was in my sights and too close for comfort. I fired a quick burst and banked away. Smoke from its engine indicated that I had caused some damage, but the plane flew on. I climbed steeply, banked and came from above for a second shot. I knew I had to move in quickly, since there were other 'Spits' around that would have loved to claim my kill. Not to be. This time I made no mistake. The Junkers exploded in the sky under my ferocious assault. There were no survivors.

We didn't have it all our way. I saw a Spitfire nose into the ground and explode on impact. Another went down; the pilot's parachute saved him. I couldn't identify the luckless pilots. I was too engrossed watching the bombers, whose formation seemed to be breaking up under the onslaught.

I saw Squadron Leader Kit Palmer on the tail of a stray Heinkel bomber. Once in his sights, he was too experienced a warrior to allow his prey to escape. I saw the flashes from his cannons and watched the Heinkel buckle under the impact. Undoubtedly its bombing days were over, but it continued to fly. The ME 109 came within attacking range on the blind side of Kit's Spitfire. I broke radio silence with an urgent warning:

"Sir – bandit on starboard side. Take evasive action. Over."

That he got the message was obvious, since his Spitfire banked over sharply to evade the predator's fire. What might have been a direct hit on the fuselage caught his starboard wing and seemed to ignite. I could see the danger of an explosion better than he. Over the intercom, I shouted hysterically, "Your wing's on fire! Abandon ship. Jump now, sir."

I knew that he had received my message. I believe I saw a wave in acknowledgement. With only seconds to spare, he manoeuvred his Spitfire within ramming distance of his assailant. I could see what was going to happen. Like a horror movie. There was nothing I could do. The two planes collided in mid-air with a huge explosion. I was temporarily blinded and stunned by the force of it. The fireball that was two aeroplanes seemed to hang in the air before falling to the ground. On the way down, the debris enveloped a further bomber, flying immediately below, which joined the downward spiral.

At this horrendous and dangerous moment, my thoughts were focused on the genial but tormented actor, whom I had only got to know moments earlier. I mouthed the words from 'Hamlet' that he would have loved to speak as his epitaph: 'Good night sweet Prince. And flights of angels sing thee to thy rest.'

If poor Kit had survived to see it, he would have drawn grim satisfaction from taking two Nazi bombers with him on his suicidal attack. Amidst the shock of it all, I could hear him saying, "Two Heinkel bombers for the life of a clapped-out old actor with only one leg... that's grand... f just GRAND."

Chapter Ten

'This is the BBC Home Service. Here is the 9.00 o'clock news on the 18th August read by Alvar Lidell.

'Today saw the heaviest air attack of the war. Twenty-three enemy aircraft are known to have been shot down and many more severely damaged. RAF losses were recorded as three shot down and one believed lost over the English Channel. Search and rescue operations are still in progress.'

Ginger and I were resting in the mess between sorties, listening to the carefully edited news. We knew the ratio of losses to kills better than the BBC. As enemy planes were destroyed, they were easily replaced. The arsenal of planes and pilots seemed inexhaustible. We were flying around the clock. No sooner was the wing on the ground with a quick cup of tea and biscuit, than a 'scramble' siren sounded for the next sortie. 'Rest' periods were often only as long as it took to re-arm and re-fuel the Spitfires. The wing, now commanded by Squadron Leader Ginger Rogers had suffered casualties, mostly 'rookie' pilots, replaced by the same. No time for extended training at this stage.

"They have to learn the hard way," Ginger commented dryly, "and that's often too damn late."

"Look at poor old Peter Jones, the Welshman. First time out. Petrified. Couldn't remember the first thing we taught him."

There was no time for further deliberations. The 'scramble' was on again.

I shouted to Maisie the mess waitress, "Keep my coffee warm… back in twenty minutes, hopefully."

'This is the BBC Home Service. Here is the 9.00 o'clock news on 23ʳᵈ August read by Bruce Belfrage.

'There has been intense enemy air activity with a number of heavy attacks on coastal airfields. The attacks failed to stop Fighter Command from taking off and harassing the bombers, whose formations broke up in disarray. Heavy casualties were inflicted on the enemy, with the loss of two planes on the ground. No casualties were reported.'

"Bloody Hell," Ginger said on listening to the BBC. "Understatement of the war! Our runways've got so many craters, I don't think we can take off any more."

"Women's Land Army has moved in. Trying to fill the holes! Keep this up and we've had it."

Fire engines and ambulances were careering around the station in the aftermath of a lethal attack.

"The BBC can't tell the enemy how bloody successful their attacks are. They'd keep them up. Grapevine has it that Biggin Hill's closed down. Ten attacks they've had. Can't move in or out."

'This is the BBC Home Service. Here is the 9.00 o'clock news on the 24ᵗʰ August read by Frank Phillips.

'Air raids have continued over the day and night. Airfields have again borne the brunt of the attacks. There has been little damage sustained and attempts to keep Fighter Command grounded have failed.'

Ginger had to be restrained from throwing his cap at the radio.

"Bloody rubbish," he shouted. "Little damage?" he quoted as he looked out of the mess window to see a runway that had as many holes as a pepper pot. "I don't think we can get in the air while it's like this."

"We're not the only ones. Hornchurch had four attacks. Think they have to close. Same at Debden and North Weald. They're going round systematically knocking out one base after another. When they've done the round, they'll start again."

"If the Germans keep up the pressure on the airfields, the Battle of Britain is over. Simple as that," Ginger concluded.

'This is the 9.00 o'clock news for the 25th August, read by Alvar Lidell.

'Bomber Command has successfully bombed Berlin.'

A huge assembled cheer rose from the assembled pilots.

"About bloody time, too. Give the bastards some of their own medicine," they echoed.

'The mission caused heavy damage to the German capital and vital installations are reported to be ablaze. Some RAF bombers failed to return.'

"They don't tell us how many. Berlin's a long way in." For a brief moment I thought about Tania and wondered whether she was safe.

Attacks on the airfields continued relentlessly. Our defence mechanism was severely impaired. The Germans must have observed that Fighter Command had lost its punch. Ginger continued to be gloomy.

"It's only a question of time," he warned pessimistically. "If they keep it up, we've had it."

I frequently tuned into the official German 'Rundfunk', to hear how they reported the battle. I picked up a Hitler speech, in which he spoke passionately about Bomber Command's raid on Berlin. He screamed at the top of his voice and the German nation cheered him. I translated for Ginger's benefit.

"The British have dared to attack our beloved capital city. That is their response to my stated policy of preserving civilian life and hitting only military targets. I now declare that this pledge, which I gave officially, is withdrawn." There were cheers from his audience.

He raised his voice to a mighty crescendo, "For every bomb that is dropped on any German city, we will respond with one thousand bombs. We will obliterate the English cities, one after another, until they plead for mercy."

Ginger commented dryly, "Let's hope the bastard keeps his word and lays off the airfields."

'This is the BBC Home Service. Here is the 9.00 o'clock news on September 7th, read by Alvar Lidell.

'Waves of enemy planes have attacked the London Docks and the East End over the last twenty-four hours. It is estimated that eight hundred bombers were involved with strong fighter support in the heaviest assault of the war so far. Fighter Command has been operational at full strength, flying non-stop sorties to break up and destroy the waves of hostile aircraft. The enemy has suffered heavy casualties and in excess of one hundred planes are thought to have been shot down. Some enemy fighters, engaged over the capital, are known to have run out of fuel and attempted to land in the Channel.'

"The nasty man has changed tack," Ginger declared confidently, "and now he'll lose the battle."

Our wing had been up and down six times in the raging battle. Between us, we must have bagged ten kills. We were fatigued beyond measure, but the adrenalin kept us going. After the fifth sortie, Ginger and I collapsed in the mess on hard wooden chairs, legs sprawled out. "Maisie, for God's sake bring us food and drink, quick. Bodies need to re-fuel as well as planes."

There were still bombers coming and we needed to intercept them fast.

"I've done two certs today, maybe three. Takes my bag to sixteen so far," Ginger boasted.

"I'll catch you. War's not over yet," I retorted.

A quick drink and sandwich still in hand, the race was on to get back in the air. Ginger was already revving up, eying the rest of the wing as they scrambled to their planes, still warm from the previous sortie. He gave a 'forward' wave and took off. At two hundred feet, his Spitfire was at its most vulnerable. The screech of a diving Stuka could be heard by all on the ground. Since it came from behind, Ginger was oblivious to the danger. Even if he had seen it coming, there was nothing he could have done about it. The Stuka dived to within one hundred and fifty feet of the target Spitfire. At such short range, his two bombs couldn't miss. He released them simultaneously and pulled out of the dive to gain altitude. Ginger didn't stand a chance. His plane became a fireball in mid-air and dropped to the ground like a stone. I witnessed the entire attack in horror. I was shaking with rage and sorrow. My dearest friend gone. My inspiration from the day we met.

But first, revenge. I had learnt that the Stukas were most vulnerable after they pulled out of a dive. As it surged upwards, I was on its tail. I got him two thousand feet up. I opened up with everything I had. The assassin plane somersaulted on impact and crashed to the ground. It wasn't going to bring Ginger back, but at least I derived some satisfaction from avenging him.

'This is the BBC Home Service. Here is the 9.00 o'clock news on 14th September read by Frank Phillips.

'The last forty-eight hours have been without air attacks. The enemy has suffered known losses of 1,885 planes during the past 57 days of conflict. There is cautious optimism that the Battle of Britain has been won. The Prime Minister, the Right Honourable Winston Churchill will address the nation after this bulletin.'

I walked from my Spitfire in a trance of disbelief. Ginger, my indestructible friend had been killed. His confidence in and out of the air had inspired the entire squadron. The great friendly rivalry that had punctuated our friendship was over. I dumped my kit on the bunk and walked to the mess.

I was embraced by our friends. They all knew how close we were. In a moment of patriotism, a single voice started to sing 'Land of Hope and Glory'. Within a moment the whole mess joined in the chorus. Followed by three rousing cheers for Squadron Leader Ginger Rogers.

Little consolation. He fought the Battle of Britain until the very last day. Therein itself lay the tragedy.

I retired to my bunk. I put my hands over my eyes and sobbed. My best mate gone. Life without him had lost its meaning. I had to get out of Spitfires. Without him there was no hope for me. That day I had lost the will to fight, even to live. My only thought was revenge.

For all he had done to my family and friends, to the whole world, my hatred was intense. So intense that I knew there was only one way for me to continue the war.

I was in a fragile state of mind. I allowed a few days to pass before I called on Suzy. She had already digested the news.

We touched cheeks. Our tears mingled.

"I am so, so sorry," I said, as if taking full responsibility for the fearful event.

"I knew it would happen, just knew it," she sobbed.

I held her hand and pushed it to my chest.

"Darling Suzy," I said, "his life was short, but every day counted. He loved his flying. Nothing could stop it. Like the force of an avalanche."

"I loved him so much, so very much," she said with uncontrollable tears.

"And he you. Talked about you all the time," I consoled her.

"Did he really? He never once told me he loved me."

"Well, that was Ginger wasn't it. We loved each other too – but neither of us ever showed it. We were like brothers."

This made her cry even more. I put my arms around her and hugged her.

In this moment of acute distress, her powder-free face, even though covered in the moisture of her tears, looked sublimely beautiful. I continued to clutch her hand.

I spoke with confidence. "I have a plan. I'm going to avenge Ginger!" This was the defining moment. "I'm going to kill Hitler."

She expressed concern for my survival. This was to haunt me in the hardships that lay ahead.

Chapter Eleven

As part of the 'Masterplan', I decided to explore the whereabouts of Bomber Command, newly based at RAF High Wycombe. It presented a good opportunity to take my new toy on its first run.

I felt comfortable at the wheel of Ginger's MG. It reminded me of him. Its bright red colour always attracted attention. I stopped at some lights quite near to the RAF station. In front of me, a black official-looking Wolseley. Being stationary, I thought it safe to glance at the card Ginger had left in the glove compartment. I had to smile. With typical Ginger cynicism, he had written: *'To my Best Mate. Please look after my baby. Hopefully drive her better than your Spit. Good luck.'*

Inexperienced as I was, I shouldn't have taken my eye off the road. I was riding the clutch waiting for green, when my foot slipped and the powerful MG catapulted into the car in front. Both drivers emerged to meet face to face. He was shaking with rage; I was apologetic. I saw to my horror that I had struck the car of a high-ranking RAF officer. An Air Marshal, no less.

I fumbled a half-salute, realizing that I was hatless.

"Don't bother with formality, laddie," were his first angry words.

"I'm so sorry, sir," I stuttered, "my foot slipped the clutch."

"I can believe it. What, in God's name, were you thinking about, laddie?"

"I am thinking now, sir, that of all the people to crash into, why did it have to be the highest-ranking officer I have ever had the misfortune of addressing under such circumstances. I am truly sorry, sir." I noticed he wore heavy-rimmed spectacles and a bristly moustache. A flicker of a smile crossed his face.

"Never mind, laddie. It'll give the insurance wallers something to think about."

We examined our cars to evaluate the extent of the damage. The Wolseley's bumper was broken and the boot had a nasty dent. The MG had left a streak of red paint at the point of contact. I rubbed it to see if it could be removed, unsuccessfully, then turned to look at the MG. The front had been buckled and was steaming. I tried the starter. It turned sluggishly, but no more than that.

"Looks like I'll have to leave her here," I suggested, trying to sound cheerful.

"Well, I have to get to the office right now. Have an important call coming in, so I can't hang about." I could do no more than apologise again.

"Haven't got the time to take details now, laddie, so best come to my office and let my secretary make the arrangements." I said that would be fine, the least I could do. It looked as though I might be getting a free lift right to the place I was planning to visit. Once sitting beside him, he introduced himself.

"I'm Arthur Harrison," he said. "Air Officer in command of No. 5 Group." I recognised the same WW1 decorations worn by Kit Palmer, but my new acquaintance came with far superior credentials.

"Sir," I said humbly, "I would far rather have met you under better circumstances, but I'm Flying Officer Peter Wolf." We shook hands.

"You fly Spits?" he said. I nodded. "You've done a great job. I think Jerry feels the pain. Hasn't paid us any visits these past few weeks."

I could see he was in a hurry to catch up for lost time. As he crunched into first gear, I thought it best to talk about the Battle of Britain, so that perhaps I could convince him I was better at flying Spitfires than I was driving cars.

"I came through unscathed," I said, "with about 12 kills. The saddest thing was the death of my best friend and mentor, whose car I am taking out on its maiden voyage with very unsatisfactory results, as you have seen."

He smiled, I thought I was forgiven. His anger seemed to have abated, now that he was back on the road, driving rather swiftly to his destination.

"What brings you to this part of the world?" he enquired, pleased to put the incident behind him.

"Well sir, I was thinking of applying to join Bomber Command."

"Very unwise," he commented and repeated. "Very unwise indeed if you value your life, that is. Every raid carries a near 50% loss risk."

"Yes, sir, I understand. But the desire to give the enemy back a bit of what they've given us is paramount. I have a lot of avenging to do," I said bitterly. "The brilliant attack on Berlin sparked all manner of ideas." I wasn't going to disclose my plan to him or anyone else for that matter.

"It was a tactical attack, no more than that. Very little damage done and expensive. Ninety-seven planes set off; only 40 came back. But it's a start and shows Hitler that his cities are not immune from being hit. He has the philosophy that he can bomb at will – but no-one can attack him."

"Hopefully, I may be with you in time for one of your future raids." Having done his best to deter me, he smiled at my on-going persistence.

The Headquarters of Bomber Command loomed ahead of us. A barrier manned by two NCOs brought us to a halt. The driver was identified. The NCOs stood back and saluted smartly and raised the barrier. The Wolseley had a reserved space in the car park. The Air Marshal edged in carefully, leaving enough space either side to exit comfortably.

"Look here, laddie," he said, "come to my office and allow my secretary to take details and we'll take it from there."

"Thank you very much, sir." This time, I managed to salute correctly.

He moved so quickly as to belie his years, or perhaps to emphasise the importance of his appointment. He picked up his briefcase, slammed the door of the Wolseley far harder than was necessary, didn't stop to lock it, ignored the security checkpoint on entering the building and pushed me through with 'this laddie's with me… I'll look after him'. Then half walking, half running, he guided me through a series of corridors, swing doors and two flights of stairs, until we stood in front of a door, marked 'Air Marshal Sir Arthur Harrison'.

His secretary, a pretty little WAAF in uniform, rose to greet him… I was out of breath, he apparently not.

"Has he phoned?"

"No sir."

"Thank God. He's as late as I am." He looked at an accumulation of papers and messages on his desk. He became immersed in one of them and reading it, he seemed to have forgotten I was standing there. He appeared shocked by what he read. After a while, he looked up and remembered why he had brought me there.

"Er… Betty, this is… er… er," I helped him out.

"Flying Officer Peter Wolf, 17 Squadron."

"Quite so," he said. "We had something of an altercation on the way in."

She smiled at me as though to say I was not the first to have had a little 'altercation' with her boss. "A bit of damage to both cars. Please deal with the insurance claim – there's a good girl," he threw in gratuitously.

He sat at his desk to study his mail, while Betty led me to her adjacent office. She kept it neat and tidy, giving the impression that she was not over-worked while her boss was out. The typewriter had been pushed to the back of her desk, to make way for an open copy of *Picture Post*. She seemed pleased to have company and having been given a task. She closed the magazine, sat at her desk and invited me to pull up a chair.

"Now, what you been up to, sir?" she giggled.

I told her the story, which she thought was funny.

"You're not the first." That made me feel a bit better.

"You got insurance?"

I had taken an insurance certificate from the glove compartment of the MG and put it in my wallet, assuming that I had cover. "Yes," I replied with little confidence. I handed her the certificate and gave her details of the car. Before she could take any action, the switchboard buzzed an in-coming call.

"Hello? Air Marshal Sir Arthur Harrison's office."

"The Prime Minister would like to have a word with him. Would you put him on please." She pulled a few levers. "Sir, the P.M. would like to speak to you." Now I understood the urgency of getting back to the office. He put the in-coming call on loudspeaker. Betty was looking up the insurance company's phone number. As long as she kept quiet I could faintly hear the gist of the conversation next door.

"Prime Minister, with respect, sir, have you read the 'Butt' report?"

"What's that all about then?"

"It shows that only one in three bombers gets within 5 miles of its target. Therefore, sir, if we attack only specific targets, we run a lot of risks for probably low rewards."

"So what is it you suggest?"

"Area bombing will show results. Precision bombing will not."

"Oh hello. Is that "Law Union Rock? Could I speak to someone about Policy J100756B7?"

Betty was reading from the certificate I had given her.

"Just a moment, Madame. I'll put you through to Mr Pettifor."

I cursed as she spoke, since I could no longer eavesdrop on the much more interesting conversation next door.

"Area Bombing, as you call it, I presume, shows no respect for civilian casualties. I do not wish to descend to their level of depravity."

"Sir, with respect, I will respond with only one word. Coventry. 65,000 casualties."

"I am aware of the figures, Sir Arthur. Nonetheless I find it difficult to condone the bombing of innocent civilians. Under any circumstances."

"Oh hello Mr Pettifor. I am ringing to report an accident, I hope covered by your Policy number J100756B."

"Just a moment, Madame while I turn it up?"

"Morale of the German people will become a big factor in winning the War, Prime Minister. Hitler will soon lose the adulation of his people if they are put under the same sort of pressure that we have suffered. Have they shown a shred of remorse for the people of this country? Certainly not. Why should we not retaliate with the same? Hitler thinks his cities are immune from attack. Our job on Berlin infuriated him. We have to give him more of the same. It's the only language he understands. When we get our new 'Heavies' into action, we have to pound their cities day and night."

"Oh yes, I have it now," said the indefatigable Mr Pettifor. "The name of the driver?"

"It's Flying Officer Peter Wolf."

"Just a moment, Madame, while I check up."

"You mean the new Lancasters? When do they become operational?"

"Within 2 months sir. And from then on, I want to build a force that can dispatch 1000 bombers on every raid to every German city. I want to show them that we, too, can resort to blanket bombing. Just like they did, but heavier. I assure you, sir, it will become a major factor in winning the War."

"Well here we are Madame. I am sorry to inform you that cover only exists for Mr Rogers, the vehicle's owner. He didn't insure for any other driver."

I whispered to her, "Mr Rogers died in his Spitfire defending his country."

She repeated verbatim, "Mr Rogers died in his Spitfire defending his country."

"I'm very sorry to hear it."

"Under the circumstances would you not consider an ex gratia payment? Flying Officer Peter Wolf flies Spitfires too. He's such a lovely boy."

I applauded her initiative and gave her a thumbs up.

"Wait a minute, Madame. I'll speak to my manager."

"It's a question, a vital one, sir, of breaking their morale. I beg you to give me the green light."

"You make a good argument, Sir Arthur. I'll sleep on it and call you in the morning."

"Thank you, sir."

"Hello again, Madame. No, I'm sorry. There's nothing we can do. Flying Officer Mr Wolf needed to inform us he was now driving the car to validate the policy. I'm sorry we can't help on this occasion."

The Air Marshal was flushed when he emerged from his office.

"I think I've won 'im over," he said triumphantly.

Betty wasn't too clear what it was all about. She brought him down to earth.

"Sir, I'm sorry to say that the Flying Officer has no cover."

"Wozzat all about?" He had completely forgotten the reason I was there.

Betty repeated her findings a little more elaborately. I pulled a crisp white, folded £5 note from my wallet. "It's all I have on me till next pay-day."

"Never mind that now, laddie. The Air Ministry will pay the damage."

Then he chortled happily, "I think I've won 'im over. I really do."

Seeing him in such a good mood, I reminded him of my wish to join Bomber Command.

"Don't just stand there, Betty. Give the lad an application form."

I saw in *The Times* seven days later, that Sir Arthur Harrison had been appointed 'Air Officer Commander in Chief' of Bomber Command.

I smiled when I saw that he had indeed, 'Won 'im over.'

Chapter Twelve

"Awesome," I mumbled to myself. "Bloody awesome."

My first impression on seeing an 'Avro Lancaster' in the flesh.

I was standing in its shadow, beneath the cockpit, eyeing the magnificent structure above. This monster craft looked invincible; yet by its sheer size, vulnerable. Suddenly, I longed to get back to my Spitfire. So sleek, simple, elegant – yet lethal. But above all, I could fly it. Beauty and the beast. The beast it was, I had to master.

We stood in a semi-circle, the seven of us, around Squadron Leader Dickie Miles, who was to take us on a conducted tour of the 'Beast'. He wore an eye patch over his left eye, which he told us, was a temporary affliction, caused by shrapnel on active service. "Nothing to worry about," he understated, "but there's not much demand for one-eyed pilots these days." The crew laughed politely.

The wireless operator, Jack (the Ripper) Bell said to me:

"Bloody 'ell. If you can win the Battle o' Britain single-handed like and shoot down all them Jerry planes, yer gonna be the best skipper take us there and back safely."

In Civvy Street, he ran a radio repair shop in the East End. The others seemed to concur. We were now on the final phase of our training, known as OTU – Operational Training Unit.

"Time we got started." The Squadron Leader led the way to mid-fuselage. A hatch opened at the push of a button and steps unwound inviting us aboard. Not a friendly welcome. We had to crouch and squeeze through a very low and narrow passageway to the pilot's cockpit.

"This is a new design," our mentor told us proudly. "Hellova lot better than the original. Designer by the name of Roy Chadwick. A brilliant fellow."

"Blimey," said Fred Loader, volunteer rear gunner. "Did 'e 'ave bloody midgets in mind?"

"Steady on," said Lofty Woodhouse, the 5' 2" mid-turret gunner.

"Sorry mate," came the reply. "No offence intended." The crew laughed.

Crossing the spar, as it was identified to us, was quite an athletic feat in the cramped conditions.

"Supports the wing span either side," explained our mentor. "Can't live without it, I'm afraid. The wings would fall off and we wouldn't get very far without them," he added cynically.

"A lot of fun if you're in a hurry to get out quickly and you have to get over that lot," observed bomb aimer Micky Myers.

We squeezed into the cockpit. I sat at the controls for the first time and studied the vast panel of gauges, dials and switches.

"Blimey O'Riley," said Fred Loader. "Hope you can understand that little pile."

Little Lofty Woodhouse said, "Blow me down with a feather. Wouldn't know where to begin."

Actually, the simulator I had learnt on, appeared very accurate and I had no difficulty identifying the gadgets and what they did.

"This is new," said the Squadron Leader. "You have a fire extinguisher for every engine. Push the button and the fire's out. But beware – the fuel's in the wings and if it spreads, you'll be toast for tea!" Polite laughter. "Now this is where the wireless operator sits, facing forward, beside the navigator."

Jack and Johnnie quietly took their seats to sort out their equipment. I stayed at the controls to try and get the feel of it all, after weeks on the simulator.

Having seated three of his crew, our mentor carried on:

"Sitting next to the pilot on his right, is the Flight Engineer."

Paddy Murphy, the soft spoken Irishman from Belfast, moved forward to take up his position on a folding seat. He was a former mechanic, a wizard of all technical data ranging from fuel gauges to booster pumps.

Apologetically the Squadron Leader explained, "Not the most comfortable of seats, I'm afraid, but it has to be folding to allow the bomb-aimer to get through."

By way of explanation, Mick Myers, the sharpest eye in town, unseated the engineer to access his post. Known as the 'goldfish bowl', it was designed to give him the best view. He had to lie flat on his tummy, propped up by an adjustable support. He had already learnt how to fuse the bombs before detonation and was also familiar with the selection panel. His instruction had covered the programming of speed and altitude into a Vector type machine. This would produce two lines of light on a screen. Where they crossed, the bomb would strike. He had to talk to the pilot to reach that point. Lovingly he massaged the button he would have to press at the right moment.

"Release the bombs, get a hit, and off home a bit sharpish. Easy."

"Bloody easy – as long as you don't miss Micky," said Johnnie, the navigator.

"Don't know the meaning of that word – but if I do, not likely, all we do is go round again."

"Let's not go down that route," I said from the cockpit.

"Have confidence, Gentlemen – I'll not let you down," said Micky. He changed the subject. "Best spot up here," he observed prosaically. "If things don't work out I'll be first one out."

"Fine," interrupted the Squadron Leader, "but in your haste to save number one, don't forget to turn behind you here." He indicated the spot. "Grab your parachute and clip it on. Without it, you'll be first on the ground that's for sure."

Micky said his memory was not that good, but he would try 'very hard' not to forget.

"Another thing you have to remember, Micky is this. You only have to slip into your bomb-aiming role, when you approach the target area. But until then – you'll be manning the front turret, just behind you."

Micky tried the move. It was quite simple. "Excuse me, sir," he said seriously. "Two jobs? Do I get two lots of pay?"

"You never know your luck. Try the Paymaster General. He'll be delighted to hear from you." Everyone in earshot laughed and continued to adjust to their workstations.

The tour now moved towards the tail of the craft. They struggled across the central spar and settled on the mid-turret. Lofty Woodhouse occupied the seat behind the .303 Browning machine guns. He swivelled them around, looked through the sights and fired some imaginary bursts. He looked as though he belonged there, his 5' 2" frame perfect for the small cockpit, with a view all round.

"Anything comes within range, 'e's 'ad 'is chips!"

"Well make sure he's not one of ours first," said our mentor.

"Don't worry, sir. I'll have me specs on."

"I'm sure you will. Anyway, if you need to use your nearest exit, it's via the same hatch we came in through." He pointed mid fuselage. "So it's not far. Remember you pick up your parachute just behind you and clip it on. You'll have the chance to experiment with all this on your dummy run."

"Can't wait," said Lofty tinged with sarcasm. He stayed playing with his new toys, while Fred Loader moved apprehensively to his post of 'tail-end Charlie'.

"I'm not going to mince my words," the Squadron Leader began with a suspicion of an apology, "but this is the most exposed position in the aircraft. It is also the most important." He paused, allowing the first statement to sink in. "Any aerial attack is likely to come from behind. Your job is to keep the captain totally informed of what you see. You are his eyes. You must inform him how many fighters are attacking you, their approximate height and speed, so that he can take evasive action if necessary. They are unlikely to be of friendly intent and you have four Brownings to get them before they get you."

"Sounds a dangerous place to be," Fred observed nervously.

"I prefer to call it 'exposed'. You're on your own to a certain extent. You won't see the rest of the crew until you're safely back home. Depending on where the target is, could be 10-12 hours."

Fred shuddered visibly on receipt of this information.

"Sounds like I picked a real good 'un. Should have listened to what me Dad told me – 'never volunteer for nothing'. Should have kept me big mouth shut."

"It's not like that at all," the Squadron Leader said reassuringly. "You're all part of a team, working together to hit Jerry hard, give him a bloody nose and come back safely."

"Thanks sir. I'll try to remember that stuff. Just in case, sir, where's my nearest exit?"

"Ah good. I was coming to that," he replied effusively. "You are rather fortunate in a way, because you have your very own private escape route."

Fred had all but switched off. He couldn't take in more information.

"It's never pleasant to talk about such eventualities. But we have to be realistic and know what to do in extreme circumstances." The information was falling on deaf ears.

"You see these flap doors here," he pointed, not sure whether Fred did. "Well what you do is to slide them open, like so; then swivel the turret around like so." He demonstrated. "Now you're facing outwards and the gun inwards. It's quite easy really. Then you just drop out."

Fred was looking white. He muttered to himself, "Must have been mad to go for this little job – stark, raving mad."

The squadron Leader had nearly done.

"The parachute's just behind you. Clip it on before you slide the flaps open… And just another thing… put your thermals on… gets quite chilly in here… no heating, you know."

I went over each dial, gauge and lever, speaking its purpose out loud, the better to memorise the data. Then I put life into each of the engines in turn. The Rolls Royce Merlins rose to the occasion. Their combined roar was deafening as revolutions increased. At full throttle, the craft shook under its imposed power.

I would have liked to take her off the ground, but that had to wait until our scheduled maiden flight that night. After a few experiments, I switched off the power. As the engines died down, the silence was eerie.

It was time for us to vacate the craft. We walked around the plane externally, to get an outside view of what we had seen inside. Its logo, boldly printed on the top of the fuselage had already been disproved, 'No enemy plane will ever fly over the Reich. Hermann Göring'.

Mike Myers said, "I can't wait to get you Mr Fatty Göring and wipe that smile off your face."

We were studying the tail fins, looking up at tail-end Charlie's turret from the ground. Its four Browning .303 machine guns looked ominous for any predators. Fred Loader, its intended occupant was standing beside me.

"A bit scary, isn't it," he stated nervously. "So cut off from the rest of the crew. Like fighting a war all on me own. Don't know if I can handle it… I really don't. I'm shit scared and that's the honest truth, Governor. Don't think I can do it."

I put my arm around his shoulder to reassure him.

"We're all shit scared, but that doesn't stop us doing our job."

I reminded him how enthusiastic he had been in training and what a shame it would be to give up now.

"We've become strong together and we're going to fly this thing together – successfully. We're all nervous, that's natural, but we gain strength in each other's company."

"Thanks," he replied sullenly. "You're a good skipper and I trust you. I just hope I won't let you down."

I squeezed his shoulder affectionately. "We'll be fine," I said with as much confidence as I could muster.

We had completed the full circle of the Lancaster and joined the rest of the crew, waiting to be addressed by our mentor.

"Gentlemen, you have now become acquainted with the most powerful flying machine the world has ever know. If Messrs. Hitler and Göring had had the benefit of such a magnificent weapon, the outcome of the 'Battle of Britain' might well have been different. We carry a potential bomb-load of 20,000 pounds and German industry will soon feel the pressure of the pounding we intend to inflict upon it. Our boss, the head of Bomber Command, Sir Arthur Harrison" – I smiled at the memory of my crash acquaintance – "predicts that the systematic bombing of German industrial capacity will ultimately destruct their war production and crush the morale of the people. In time we will fly over 7000 of these fantastic bombers to do the job. We will mount 1000 bomber raids on a nightly basis. Gentlemen, you are privileged to take the war into Hitler's back yard and pound him into submission. And that is the aim for us all."

The crew was clearly impressed if not overawed by these words of patriotism and encouragement.

Now the Squadron Leader would give us further details of the schedule:

"Tonight you will fly a dummy raid on a given target within the British Isles. I will be on board as an observer and believe me, my one eye will not miss a trick. I will then preside over a de-brief. Any errors or irregularities will be scrutinised. If I consider it necessary, we will fly a second dummy run. Hopefully, for their own sakes, we will not have the pleasure of encountering any enemy planes, but if we do, the Brownings will be loaded and ready for action. So gunners, be prepared and alert. The British nation is to be spared the threat of live bombs being dropped on it, but I will want to see all the procedures in operation." Polite laugher. "Any questions, so far?" Silence. "Now, you will want to know what happens after tonight's little excursion. This team will split up and each of you will be seconded to an operational crew that will have gained some experience. Thereafter, hopefully you will re-assemble as a successful and confident crew. We operate a tour rota which comprises 30 Sorties. Once completed, you may apply for a spot of leave. Is that OK with everyone?" He paused for queries or questions. There were none. "Very well then. We meet tonight at 2100 hours in full flying kit for target briefing, ready for take off at 2200 hours. Thank you and good luck."

Chapter Thirteen

The dummy run went surprisingly well. The crew 'gelled' as though veterans. The exception was Fred Loader. Our 'tail-end Charlie' took no part in the exercise, either by way of communication or playing out the role of shooting at imaginary attackers. He looked pale and distraught as we landed. He made no contribution to the de-briefing. Nor did he attend a celebration of our maiden flight at the 'Bull and Bush'.

I found a personal note from him under my pillow that night saying he could not carry on. "I am too worried about letting you and the team down. Sorry," he wrote. I never saw or heard from him again. I know what his fate would have been in WW1.

But out of bad there is sometimes good. So it was with our new rear gunner. A lovely boy turned man at the age of 18. He was studying medicine at Cambridge, cruelly interrupted by the War in his first year. A total opposite to his predecessor, he was fearless. He accepted the duties of rear gunner with full optimism and not a moment's thought for his safety. There was even excitement when he swivelled the gun turret around to practise escape if it ever became necessary. His name was Tom Rosefield and we were to become very close friends.

On mission number three, he got the action he craved. On the way home after a successful raid on the Ruhr, Tom reported four ME 109s on our tail. He held fire until they were close enough to guarantee a hit, then fired. Lofty Woodhouse did the same from the mid-turret. Between them they had the joy of taking out two of the fighters, the two remaining climbed to attack from above. Guns blazing, they inflicted severe damage to the Lancaster. I had to deal with two engines on fire. The extinguisher worked, but the engines were knocked out. Not only that, but I guessed the tail fins had been shot to bits, since I couldn't bank the aircraft and could only fly straight. This was a pilot's worst nightmare. Flying on two engines over enemy territory. Lofty Woodhouse had paid a terrible price for his defiance. His turret had been blown out of the sky and he was missing, presumed dead. If he had to go, then this was the way he would have wished it to happen.

We limped to the Channel, losing altitude and I was relieved to see Spitfires overhead which removed the threat of German fighters finishing us off. Jack's wireless had been sending out Mayday messages since the attack and here was Fighter Command's response. The ME 109s beat a hasty retreat and no more was seen of them.

Never before had the White Cliffs of Dover given such a luminous glow of welcome, as we passed them in the black of night. I prayed that the working engines would get us down safely. We made a one-sided, bumpy landing. The plane listed dangerously to port side and a flotilla of fire engines and ambulances surrounded our plane and sprayed it both sides to prevent fires from spreading. Of my crew, one was dead and Paddy Murphy was severely injured, brave young men who had given their lives to the destruction of Adolf Hitler. My resolve to get him was greater than ever. They gave us a 48-hour pass after that episode. Then invited us to a special briefing for Mission number four.

Squadron Leader Dickie Miles was on the podium flanked by two large photographs and a close-up map of the target area.

This was the first time I had seen him without his eye-patch. From the fourth row, the uncovered eye had a strange disconnected look about it. When I got close I could see it was a glass eye. What a brave, modest man, I thought, when I recalled his reference to a 'temporary minor affliction'. What a contrast, Fred Loader.

He turned to face his blown-up pictures.

"Our target for tonight is here," he pointed his stick dramatically at the French city of Bordeaux, busy harbour town on the western coast of France. "Sorry to disappoint you, Gentlemen – not the wine industry nor even the vineyards," he got a little nervous laughter, "but here." He pointed his stick at a large building standing on the estuary of the River Garrone, not far from the Atlantic Ocean. The blow-ups showed a bird's eye view and one from the sea.

"Looks like some sort of hangar," said a pilot. "What's inside it?"

"The simple answer to that question is 'submarines'. Sixteen of them if we count bays."

There was a collective gasp from the pilots, as they understood the importance of the mission.

Dickie Miles gave us background information. "We have to win the Battle of the Atlantic to survive and we're not doing well at the moment. Our shipping lines are under constant attack from packs of submarines, operating from France and Germany. You will understand, Gentlemen, that every sub we destroy is a prize worth fighting for. Here we might kill 16 with one shot."

At this point Dickie paused to take refreshment. "Don't worry, lads. Only water."

He continued, "The average sub has to refuel every four months. They need a base with access to the Atlantic, the Med., from which they can target our shipping through Suez and the Cape, as well as the Atlantic. So there we have it, the perfect location – Bordeaux. Our enemies have seized the moment to construct a massive U boat shelter. The exact location can be seen on the blow-ups."

The crews moved across to inspect the site at close quarters.

"Our photographic team has been busy, as you can see. My information is that the walls and roof may be 12 feet thick. Only direct hits will penetrate. Follow the river and go in as low as you dare. Squadron Leader Bill Masters will lead the attack and he will go into details with you when I have finished. Just remember this: there are 16 bays inside the building, of which we believe 10 are

71

occupied at the moment. To knock them out with one blow would be a magnificent reward for this operation. We believe that the notorious U178 is there as we speak and revenge for gunning down the survivors of a warship they torpedoed, would be a very sweet act of retribution."

The assembled crew voiced their approval.

"The German War effort will be severely reduced if we can destroy this vital base and with it a pack of subs. Precision bombing adds to the dangers, but I am convinced that six of our Lancasters manned by the pick of our crews, can do the job. You will have fighter support, so your main threat will come from the ground. Take-off will be at 2400 hours, which will catch the buggers in the middle of the night and hopefully disturb their beauty sleep. Good luck everyone."

Dickie Miles had set the scene. He retired to an available seat in the first row. Now it was the turn of Jim Masters to put 'flesh on the bones'. Jim didn't have a classy background, but he was a brilliant aerial tactician. He would make an excellent leader of our mission. He tweaked his moustache, stood before the crews and said, "Right lads… this is what we're gonna do…"

Chapter Fourteen

By 2330 hours the six Lancaster bombers were ready to go, engines idling away. It would be a long, nervous and agonizing wait. Every minute seemed like an hour.

I was chewing gum, a habit I had cultivated from my Spitfire days. I passed the packet around. Evidently I was the only one in the cockpit who drew relief from jaw movement. I busied myself with the checklist, testing that all equipment responded to the lights, gauges and levers that showed up on my panel. To kill time, I went through the list three times and could find no fault. The crew was similarly engaged in preparation. Earphone music helped jittery nerves to unwind. The inevitable Vera Lynn gave us strength with a mix of Jack Hylton, Joe Loss and Artie Shaw. The intercom was open, but little communication passed.

I studied the weather reports. The half moon was hidden behind thick cloud with intermittent drizzle. Just our luck, it looked as though the target area was clear. Cloud protection would have been safer.

I checked my watch incessantly. At zero minus five, the engines were put on full throttle and we took up our position.

At zero minus one, Jim Masters broke intercom silence.

"OK lads, ready to go. This is it. Good luck everyone. Let's see whether we can blow a hole in that fucking sub-base."

His was lead plane and he took off at the stroke of midnight.

Chapter Fifteen

We flew low over the Ocean to escape RADAR detection.

The flight was uneventful; only that within 20 minutes of ETA (Estimated Time of Arrival), the unwelcome sight of cloud break-up was replaced with feathery wisps. A half-moon gave us light that we could well have done without. Help us on the way in, but deprive us of cover in the vital seconds after the 'drop'.

Navigator Dicky Miller gave his first map reading. "1.5 degrees right, please Captain. ETA 12 minutes."

I gave him thumbs up to indicate message received and understood. His next contact came 7 minutes later.

"1/2 degree left. 5 minutes ten seconds to ETA. Hold steady. Drop altitude. On course to hit target not yet visible."

Now Jim Masters' timetable came into operation. Five Lancasters banked steeply over the ocean, whilst the lead, piloted by the Squadron Leader headed for the target. We, at number 2, were to give him four minutes to do the business then attack. Dicky hit the stopwatch. "3.55 minutes to hit target. Fraction of a degree left should do it."

I shouted, "Bomb doors open," with as much cool as I could muster. "Up to you now Micky. You OK?" We had two minutes to ETA. Everything now depended on the steady hand of the bomb aimer, Micky Myers. We banked towards the target. A massive explosion led us to it. Jim had scored a direct hit. We were now so low that the fumes and dense smoke deterred our vision. Micky Myers, on his stomach, was watching his screen for the lines to merge. They were close. He now took over instruction to the pilot.

"A tiny bit more right." I complied. "Now slow it," he spoke with an unnervingly calm voice. "Now 50 feet lower and we'll hit."

Any slower, we'd have stalled; any lower we'd crash. "Get on with it Micky," I mumbled to myself. Then came the quiet composed voice.

"3... 2... 1... bombs away."

The moment I heard those words, I didn't stick around. No question of staying to watch for a direct hit. My job was now to put maximum space between ourselves and the explosion. Allowing for the short drop, I had to gain altitude then bank sharply to escape the force of the huge blast that was imminent. The Lancaster rocked momentarily with the waves of the explosion.

Then came the joyful voice of the rear-gunner, Tom Rosenfeld, "Direct Hit, boys. Good shooting. Huge explosion. Never seen anything like it."

"Well done Mike," I congratulated him and closed the bomb doors.

"And you, skipper." He crawled over to the gun turret to take up his dual role. The euphoria was short-lived.

The Germans had placed their ground fire strategically. They guessed correctly that any low-flying attack would come from west to east and had their AA defences placed at the point the attacking aircraft would be at its most vulnerable. The belly of a large Lancaster, banking to gain height, is a sitting target. The clear moonlit sky made us even more vulnerable. The beam of a searchlight crossed with another. We were caught in the apex, blinded by the glare. The sky lit up with shells exploding all around us. I saw the ominous puffs of smoke from guns below, moments before the plane was rocked by a gigantic explosion.

My dials screamed at me confirming a direct hit. Johnny Gregson's last message from the mid-turret confirmed: "Fire... Fire!" The rest of the message was cut by explosions.

I knew we were doomed and had less than a second or two to get out. There was unmistakable panic in my voice as I screamed on the intercom: "JUMP! JUMP NOW!"

The plane no longer responded fully, but I managed to put her on a straight course. With trembling hands, I clipped on my parachute and was the third to drop out of the escape hatch. The laws of gravity took me earthwards. Not before anxious seconds had passed waiting for the parachute to open. The nylon balloon above me had collected enough air to slow my descent with a sharp jolt. As I drifted, there was an eerie silence. Out of the corner of my eye, I could see two other parachutes gently gliding earthwards.

We had covered too many miles to survey the on-going attack, but far to the west, a huge explosion marked the end of OAF501. I saw a fireball spiralling earthwards. I could hear myself praying that none of the crew was still aboard.

"Thank You God," I said "for getting at least three of us out safely." I didn't have the time to add to it, since suddenly the ground seemed to come from nowhere. I made contact with a mighty thump. I rose quickly to check that no bones were broken. I released the 'chute', rolled it into a ball and looked around me to survey the acres of green fields of France that beckoned an inhospitable welcome to their country. Little did I consider at that precise moment, that I could have got myself closer to my target.

Chapter Sixteen

There were hedgerows and trees dividing the fields. Instinctively, I walked towards them, seeking cover.

I blew my emergency whistle, hoping it might attract a response from a fellow fugitive. All it did was to awake the birds, who noisily left their nests, angered by the intrusion. I found what looked like a foxhole and conveniently disposed of my parachute; then retraced my steps to pull it out. The thought of suffocating some innocent creature inside it worried me. I found a ditch which would do the job as well and covered the 'chute' with foliage.

I took stock of my position. I was in enemy territory; no doubt they would send out search parties for the crew. Sooner or later I would be taken; if in uniform, a POW camp if I was lucky; if in civvies, a firing squad.

But they had to get me first and the challenge of seeking freedom headed my options. It was a mild, moonlit night. I looked at the stars, hoping for inspiration. I remember learning about the 'Great Plough' pointing one way or the other. Since I didn't know which, going either east or west didn't have much meaning. I needed to find a road or pathway that would take me away from the scene before the search party arrived. I probably had about three hours of darkness to find cover. I didn't fancy roaming the fields in daylight.

I had to keep moving fast to find civilisation, hopefully friendly. I trudged on, traversing six huge fields. Foxes fled as I disturbed them; birds flew overhead squawking, unaccustomed to seeing human life at this time of night. I was hungry, thirsty and tired when I came across a more significant sign of life. Cows, plenty of them, contentedly chewing the cud. Cows meant that not far away there had to be a cowshed. I approached one of them and addressed her in English. Could she direct me to the farmhouse? I stroked her; I have always loved cows. I noticed her over-ripe udders. I was thirsty… if only.

Following the flattened ground and copious droppings, took me to the cowshed, obviously part of the farm. Inevitably it must be linked to a road or path at some point. I crouched to explore. Two dogs acknowledged my presence with sustained barking. Luckily they were in the house. I froze and didn't move for five minutes. The barking stopped. Hopefully the beasts had gone back to sleep. The farmer might have been awoken prematurely. I had to make a move; either knock on the door, hoping he would be friendly or slide forward as silently as possible, hoping not to disturb the dogs again. I weighed up the pros and cons. Most French peasants hated the Germans and would do their best to help an allied airman on the run. But it could go wrong. Maybe a reward would be on offer for delivering an RAF officer to the invaders. As noiselessly as possible, I left the shack, planning to make a loop and approach it from the front to explore whether that might be a dog-free zone. It occurred to me that this was the sort of isolated farm a search party would ransack and I would be trapped. I reached the front of the house and saw a clapped-out old Renault standing in the drive. Stealthily I crept towards it and tried the door. It was unlocked. It was there, it seemed, for the 'borrowing'. I sat in the driver's seat and toyed with the starter. Trouble was, the noise would surely disturb the dogs and bring the farmer onto the scene.

My brain was racing as I sat there. If I got away with it, where would I be driving to? Would there be enough petrol to get me away? Would the farmer advise the authorities? I might escape the search zone, but then I might get stopped by a patrol car or a road block. It would be a hazardous drive. I sat in the car quietly deliberating the options. The decision was taken from my grasp. A double-barrel shotgun was pointing at me through the open front door of the car. Obviously it was the farmer, whom the dogs had awoken, since he confronted me in pyjamas and slippers. Mercifully he had left the dogs in the house. He must have taken in my RAF uniform, since he enquired politely:

"Bonjour Monsieur. Je peux vous aider?"

I spoke a little school French. I pointed to the RAF insignia on my jacket,

"Je suis Anglais. RAF. Mon avion…" I couldn't think of how to say 'shot down', "est tombé du ciel." I indicated with my hand the motion of a plane going down.

He understood.

"Venez avec moi, s'il vous plaît." He invited me into the farmhouse without declaring whether he was friend or foe. He still held the shotgun in a menacing position. I climbed out of the car and was marched into the front parlour of the farmhouse. It must have been built one hundred years ago. A water pump connected to a well, an open fire with logs to cook and warm. Candles for light. My host had not moved with the times.

However, he seemed to be a well-mannered man not without old-fashioned courtesy.

"Vous avez une Carte d'Identité, Monsieur?" he enquired politely.

I fumbled in the breast pocket of my battledress jacket and found my pay-book, which stated name, rank and number. He seemed satisfied and moved to a phone, standing on the table, perhaps his only compromise to modernity. He picked up the receiver and dialled a 7- digit code. For all I knew, it could have been the Gestapo.

"Bonjour Raoul. J'espère que je ne suis pas trop tôt… tu dormais, alors je m'excuse…"

That was as far as he got.

The heavy crunching of pebbles on his driveway, skidding to a noisy halt, told him he had visitors. The barking of orders told him they were Germans on a mission. The urgency indicated this was no routine visit. The farmer moved faster than I would have thought him capable.

He banged down the receiver, knelt to remove a carpet and opened a trapdoor that led below.

"Les Boches, les Boches. Venez vîte, Monsieur."

His affiliations were no longer in doubt. I descended into the total darkness of his cellar. There was no visible means of escape. I was trapped. I groped to find some old dumped tables and chairs and managed to squeeze in behind them. I heard an imperious knock on the door. The dogs, locked inside the house went berserk. Aggressive, snarling barking that would have sent most callers away. Not so the Germans. "Aufmachen. Sofort. Schnell," they shouted banging on the door at the same time.

The farmer took his time. After all, he had been awoken from his beauty sleep.

"J'ARRIVE. J'ARRIVE. Un instant," he said as he unbolted the door and allowed them access. Standing in his slippers and pyjamas, his hair dishevelled, he looked as though he was still warm from his bed. They pushed past him and he fell to the ground. The dogs were in a frenzy, barking ferociously, from behind closed doors. I heard the boots pass over me. I estimated about 12 of them.

I crouched in a corner with only a table-top and armchair for cover. Unless they physically searched the cellar I was in with a chance. I heard the guttural voice of the commander issuing his orders.

"Zwei Mann oben, zwei Mann unten und zwei draussen,"

So there were six of them plus commander. I felt for my emergency pistol, just in case I had to defend myself. I heard the commander address the farmer in a mix of German and French:

"Wir suchen, chercher, ein Engländer. Nous avons gesehen son Fallschirm, Ici tomber... Haben Sie etwas gesehen oder gehört? Vous avez vu?"

"Je m'excuse. Je ne comprends pas."

He tried again in very broken French. "Anglais Pilote tombe... oben vom Himmel."

He indicated with his hand the motion that suggested a plane going down.

"Je n'ai rien vu. Moi. Je dormais."

There was much thumping upstairs as the soldiers ransacked the place. Meanwhile the dogs were on full alert behind the kitchen doors, growling, barking, snarling with evil intent... The downstairs team tried to enter their territory. I heard the barking reach a crescendo. I suspected the soldiers had gone in. Two shots were fired. A whimper, and then silence.

The farmer did not ask permission to tend to his beloved dogs. He rushed into the adjacent room. What confronted him was his worst nightmare. His two Alsatians, lying twitching in a pool of their own blood, gushing from a single shot in the head. Lovingly he cradled each dog in turn, trying with his bare hands to quell the flow of blood. He thought for a moment he saw signs of life. Reflexes. With his pyjamas, face and hands covered in their blood, came the cruel realisation that his dogs were dead. The soldiers were claiming self-defence. They continued their search, with little respect for the corpses that lay twitching on the floor, saturated in blood. The farmer could not restrain tears as he confronted the Commander.

"Ce n'était pas nécessaire. Si vous m'aviez demandé, j'aurais..." He could not finish his sentence and broke down. The Commander turned away, showing no sympathy, mumbling something about self-defence. "Keep the savage beasts under control," he said in German, which luckily the farmer didn't understand.

Meanwhile, the soldiers entered the front door, pistols drawn, to continue their search. They knew that these old farmhouses were built with cellars. They soon located the rug concealing the trap door.

The Commander shouted, "Los. Aufmachen. Sofort." They lifted the trap door. I stopped breathing as a torch pierced the darkness. I followed it around the cellar until it came to rest on the ramshackle furniture that I was hiding behind. The farmer chose the right moment to stage an hysterical outburst.

"Pourquoi? Pourquoi avez-vous tué mes chiens?" he screamed at the Commander through his tears, beating the Commander's chest with bloody hands. The Commander used full force to shove him away. It didn't stop him from screaming in anguish, lying in a heap on the floor.

The soldier with the torch looked up at the commotion, to see his superior removing blood from his uniform and face. He rose from his position over the trap door to find a white towel and offered help. Together they attempted to clean the uniform. The white towel soon turned red. Cleaning himself up now became of greater priority than looking for a seemingly non-existent English airman.

The soldier was considering descent into the black basement, just to make sure it really was empty, when the Commander called off the search. He badly needed a shower and change of uniform.

"Genug," he ordered, discarding the blood-soaked towel. "Niemand da. Zurückziehen. Schnell. Alle raus. Sofort."

The soldier didn't bother to close the trap door. I didn't resume normal breathing until the front door slammed and I heard the vehicle crunching pebbles on the way out. The farmer put his head to the trap door and shouted down:

"Ils sont partis, les cochons."

Gingerly I surfaced, wiping cobwebs and dust from my face and uniform. I embraced the farmer to comfort him from his tragic loss and to thank him for his brilliant intervention, which had undoubtedly saved my life. The embrace turned to a hand-shake as he introduced himself.

"Je suis Marcel Dupont."

"Et moi. Je m'appelle Peter Wolf."

We hardly knew each other, yet here was a bond of true friendship. I felt sure we would meet again after the War.

I wanted to tell him how grateful I was for his magnificent 'pièce de théatre'. But lack of French made it difficult.

I felt responsible for the shooting of his beloved dogs and apologised as well as my French would allow. Tearfully he embraced me in forgiveness. Then offered me breakfast.

I told him that would be more than welcome. First he had to make a phone call. I knew enough French to understand that his contact would be expecting us at 10.00 p.m.

After cleaning myself up, Marcel dressed himself for the day. Dirty milk-stained trousers, a striped shirt with a red silk scarf around his neck. Then breakfast. It took far too long and I was tantalised by delicious aromas that emanated from his open log fire. He laid the table and finally presented the most delicious meal I had ever tasted. Fried farmhouse eggs, jambon and tomatoes, toast, butter and coffee.

When the first pangs of hunger had been satisfied, he told me that Raoul, whom we were to visit that night, was an important member of the Resistance. He would help me with accommodation and possible escape. But first, the need to discard my uniform and become a local. I realised it meant a firing squad rather than a POW camp if things went wrong. But I was now in their hands and had to play by their rules. Obviously this car journey, destination unknown, couldn't have an RAF officer sitting in the passenger seat.

He offered me a free run of his limited wardrobe. I examined each of his unwashed trousers and selected a pair of black cords that had the least aroma attachment. They were too big by far over the waist, but had the advantage of attached red braces, which kept them in position. A red shirt seemed to fit quite well and I found a light black sweater which hid most of the misfits.

"Ça va très bien," he beamed at me as I reluctantly handed him my uniform.

We decided that it would be safest to burn it.

As dawn broke, we had the gruesome task of burying the dogs. I helped Marcel dig a deep single grave. Then he gently lifted each dog in turn and placed it lovingly into the fresh earth, legs intertwined. Giant tears ran down his cheeks as he bade his last farewell. We filled in the hole and Marcel planted a flower to mark the spot. We stood silent for a moment, heads bowed. Then Marcel said a little prayer talking to the dogs as if they were still alive. "You did your duty, you died for France."

By then, I, too, was choking with tears. I found a handkerchief. Marcel and I embraced again. Two grown men in tears over the death of the dogs. I may have been crying, but my resolve was fortified.

My 'avenge' list had grown again.

Chapter Seventeen

The farmer and his new best friend sat in the front of the old Renault by 8 p.m. Daylight was fading. A two-hour journey lay ahead. On the third attempt the engine was coaxed into life.

"Ça fait longtemps," the farmer apologised for its poor response. It didn't sound capable of going round the corner at that moment, let alone a 100 mile trip 'aller et retour'. But after initial hesitation, it seemed to manage a more or less steady tone. I was concerned to see thick smoke pouring from the exhaust. I thought to myself, 'Thank God I hadn't attempted to "borrow" it.' The noise would have terrified me and I now observed that the tank was empty. Marcel had lined up four cans of petrol, two of which went into the tank. The other two in the back of the car for the return journey. Some petrol was spilt and the fumes were nauseating, not helped by the stench of a Gauloise, as Marcel lit up before the off. He explained that petrol was at a premium and he only got his ration, because of his farm tractor, deemed essential to carry on his business and provide produce for the Germans.

Puffing away amid the vile smell, he said, "Alors, on y va," and the engine seemed ready to prove it could do the job. Mercifully he unwound a window a fraction, which allowed the combined fumes to escape. I could sense it would be an uncomfortable trip.

On leaving the farm, we turned into a narrow driveway that led to a country lane. It wasn't much wider, barely adequate for two-way traffic without careful negotiation. Luckily there were few cars on the road in the fading light. Petrol rationing had its advantages.

Marcel was very secretive about their destination, just in case I was ever questioned. I couldn't reveal what I didn't know. I was on the lookout for signposts, not that the names of villages would have meant much to me. I spotted one that said Libourne 12 kilometres and was none the wiser.

Conversation was sparse, partly the noise of the engine, but more the language connection. I was left with my thoughts over the last 24 eventful hours. The last flight... had we destroyed the base...? How many of my crew had survived...? Where might they be now...? What did the future hold for me...? Escape...? Killing Hitler...? How lucky I was to have found Marcel. Where would I be without him? Anyway, I was alive and had a new set of clothes to cherish. They had been put to good use that afternoon, since I had helped Marcel round up the cows and worked with him, trying to extract milk from their udders. The first pull was quite easy, but then he had to take over and finish them. I love cows, their rural smell. It was a relaxing and pleasant way to pass the time and not without its funny moments as I learnt the trade. I smiled as I reflected on the lighter side of the day.

We were moving at quite a steady pace now, but slowed down as we approached Libourne. I could see it was a larger town with shops, a church and a railway station. I hoped it was not large enough to warrant any occupation forces. The streets were empty. Marcel cruised through at a steady 30 mph and ejected the fag end that had been smouldering on his lower lip for the last few minutes; then promptly lit another. I noted a signpost pointing to Bergerac and the car swung over in its direction.

Thinking about the last 24 hours without any sleep, suddenly caught up on me. I felt very tired. My eyes must have closed. Marcel reached behind him for a rug and unfolded it for my benefit. I thanked him for his consideration and fell fast asleep.

It must have been the cobblestones that awoke me. The car shook as it climbed steep, narrow streets with tall antiquated houses on either side and beautiful countryside below. I later discovered that this was the medieval, historic town of Monflanquin, built on a mountain to protect against invaders.

Germans included – they had not yet penetrated this deep. The houses, 500 years old or more, stood as built, unchanged and well preserved. Most looked occupied. A tranquil, historic place, as yet untouched by the horrors of World War 2.

Marcel knew his way around. The road had taken us to the highest point. We passed a magnificent, massive cathedral at the summit and now we were freewheeling downhill. Two miles down, we found a rocky path signposted 'Calviac'. A bumpy ascent took us to an intimate, miniature church with a small cemetery on its left and the remains of what might have been a presbytery on its right. Its walls were no more than three feet high, surrounding a deep crater. The church had remained intact. It was not too dark to admire the beautiful panorama below us. If this was Resistance HQ, they had chosen well. We entered the small church, seemingly unused by worshippers, through large oak doors that were locked, but opened from the inside at the sound of a recognisable knock.

Five men were sitting in the pews, facing each other, two of them smoking irreverently. Jesus Christ on the cross above was assailed by a transient band of smoke. They rose as we walked in. They all looked the same, dressed in typical French peasant clothing similar to my own. One of them looked familiar, but out of context, there was no instant recognition in the dim church lighting. Introductions were made. We all shook hands.

"Good evening, Peter," said the one in perfect English, removing his beret. Of course, without it, I recognised him at once. The joy at meeting my rear gunner, Tom Rosefield, was boundless. We embraced, touched cheeks, French style, hugged each other again in a genuine expression of joy and happiness amid all the anxiety we had endured in reaching this desolate meeting place. In the hands of total strangers, who professed to be our friends.

Before any serious business could be discussed, we had to exchange escape stories. Tom had dropped in a tree and needed help to be cut down. A young girl, passing by, saw his plight and went to fetch her father. He duly arrived with steps and cutters. Within the hour he was on the way to Calviac and had already made friends with the Resistance fighters when I arrived. I had always liked 'fearless' Tom, although I had never really got to know him. That was about to change. Raoul introduced himself as leader of the group and as a token of friendship offered me a swig of a communal bottle of Cognac that was passing from one to the other. It was his job to look a typical Frenchman, so as not to stand out in a crowd. In this he succeeded. A collarless shirt, beneath an unbuttoned waistcoat and a dirty-looking scarf around his neck.

He had the sharp features of a squirrel, furtively looking around him for any signs of danger. He was obviously an educated man, since he addressed the meeting in reasonable English with heavy French intonation.

"It is an unexpected pleasure to welcome you here, mes amis, although pleasure is, perhaps, not the right word, from your point of view. It is good that you are still alive and well and we will do our very best to allow you to keep fighting our enemies. We are engaged in that task ourselves and we work hard to keep the pigs as occupied as ever. Malheureusement, they have a nasty habit of taking reprisals against innocent civilians every time we hurt them. Prisoners are taken and deported. We suffer casualties and know they do not treat us nicely when captured. I tell you all this, mes amis, so that you know the risks. You have been bombing them from the sky. On the ground it's difficult for us… très difficile."

The three other Frenchman spoke little or no English. As Raoul paused in reflection, one of them said, "Je n'ai rien compris… pas un mot," the other two chimed in, "moi non plus."

Raoul reassured them, "J'expliquais à nos amis les difficultées de la Résistance. Il faut apprendre un peu l'Anglais, mon ami."

They laughed heartily at the impossibility of such a suggestion.

Tom spoke next. "What do you have in mind for us to be doing here and what chance of escape?"

"Ah, mes amis, this is a big question. I am in touch with London and if you will be kind enough to give me your name and number, I will communicate that you are safe for the moment and ask their wishes."

Tom and I wrote our details on the same piece of paper and handed it to him.

"For the time being," he went on, "you can join us in our war, if you wish." He paused to allow for maximum effect. "If you will help us, we will help you."

I explained that we hated the invaders every bit as much as they did. Having survived the 'Battle of Britain' we were anxious to hurt the German war effort on the ground, to the best of our ability. Tom endorsed these thoughts. "The same goes for me," he said.

Even those who didn't speak English seemed to have understood. There was applause and general back-slapping. Tom and I were offered cheek-to-cheek embraces and an undeclared vow of friendship and camaraderie. Cigarettes were lit and a new Cognac bottle was opened and passed around.

"My English friends, I ask you. How do you see your future role in this war?"

He translated the question for his friends and my reply.

"I cannot speak for Tom, only for myself. I have an aim, a target, a challenge. Something I have built up over the past months, when I have lost so many of my friends. I have sworn vengeance. I will not rest until I achieve my dearest wish – or die in the attempt."

I paused, realising I had said too much to deny the full disclosure.

"Alors, quest-ce que c'est, mon ami? What is it you want to do?"

"I want to kill Hitler," I said unflinchingly.

They all looked at another with a mixture of surprise and delight.

Raoul said, "This we all want. But HOW?"

I replied with more confidence than I was entitled, since I had no idea as to how.

"Get me to Berlin," I said bravely, "and I'll show you."

Chapter Eighteen

We assembled at the same location seven days later. Marcel was there as well. He greeted me with a double bear hug and expressed pleasure that I was looking well and relaxed after the ordeal.

For reasons of security, Tom and I were billeted in different houses near to one another. Basement rooms in the 15th Century houses that stood ancient but well-preserved on either side of the steeply ascending cobble streets that led to the cathedral. The owners were sympathetic but were not informed of our 'provenance'. Tom and I met daily at one of the various bar/bistros to discuss the War, and what future part we could play in winning it. For exercise and entertainment we went for long walks over the magnificent countryside.

We each had a wireless in our room which received a crackly but audible BBC. We knew that our enemies were in headlong retreat in Russia and in the Middle East. Air raids on German cities were increasing by the day. America now in the war was clearly swinging the action in our favour.

Communication with our Resistance friends was strictly by word of mouth. We hadn't seen them again since our last meeting and now awaited our fate.

Formalities were quickly dispensed and after general hand-shaking and hugs, we settled in the same pews facing each other.

"You have fine lodgings?" Raoul enquired.

"Yes, we're OK," I replied, "but we want to get on with things."

"That is why we meet now, n'est-ce pas?" He looked at some notes before continuing.

"We have been busy, I assure you."

One of the other men, Colline, spoke in French slowly for our benefit. He needn't have bothered, since Raoul translated.

"We were impressed by your wish to kill Hitler. This is what we all want and 'Quel coup ça serait'," he lapsed into French. "We talk much about how we get you to Berlin and what you will do when you get there."

I thought this was a good time to disclose my credentials and play my trump card. "I am bi-lingual." Raoul translated for the others not to miss my important statement. "My father is English and my mother is German Jewish. I grew up with both languages."

I detected a slight air of hostility. So I hastened to explain that my mother despised the Germans quite as much as any Frenchman and had to suffer lost relatives in concentration camps. Tom entered the dialogue by telling the party what a valiant role I had played in the Battle of Britain, now flying Lancasters and bombing Germany. There could be no doubt of my integrity. The look of hostility on their faces gradually receded, but I refrained from informing them that I spent my adolescence in Berlin and knew my way around the city very well indeed. All valid reasons why my mission there was not as futile as they might have thought. Raoul told the Frenchmen he had full confidence in my integrity. Colline, the chief agitator apologised, "Alors, je m'excuse, mais on ne sait jamais."

The little incident was soon forgotten. Embraces, French style followed and we were all friends again. Cigarettes were lit, and the familiar Cognac bottle was passed around.

Raoul came quickly to the point. "We have a friend who flies a cargo plane each day from Bordeaux to Berlin. We trust him enough to take you on board, probably in a crate." I shuddered at the thought; no way acceptable. I said nothing. "We have to pay him of course. He will let you leave the crate once in the air and when you arrive, you go your way as you choose."

He translated into French and I replied in English. "We are very grateful to have found such good friends here and thank you all for all your good work for us. When we have killed enemy number one I hope you will have a smile on your faces and remember that without your help, it could never have happened."

Raoul translated; the Frenchman applauded. But the meeting was far from over. Raoul continued:

"Perhaps you recall when we last met, I said, 'We will help you, if you help us'."

"Bien sûr," I responded, which they all understood.

"I have to inform you that your raid did not meet with success. You hit directly but alas, you left only craters where the bombs landed, without breaking the roof. You see, mes amis, the Germans built it six metres thick for protection against the bombs, and zero serious damage was achieved."

This was the first time Tom and I heard that we had failed and paid a heavy price. We were informed later that a second Lancaster had been shot down, they thought, without survivors.

"So you see, mes amis, it is a job started but not finished. The submarines go in and out under our noses." He paused not quite sure if he had hit the right expression. "We would like to stop this. Now I ask you, mes amis, do you know what a 'Limpet' is?"

I remembered reading about a 'Limpet' mine attack, when some marines canoed sixty miles down the Gironde River and sunk some German ships using them.

Raoul was releasing more information on the subject. "Some marines were killed on the way, but those that got through, planted their magnetic mines and sunk many ships. So it was very well-done finallement. The bombs have to be attached below the water-line by divers."

Tom caught on very quickly. "So you send a party of divers to knock out the subs. Is that it?"

"How you say – easy said, but hard to do. Now, I have been in touch with SOE, that is 'Special Operations Executive' and we now have in our warehouse four Limpet bombs for some brave men to attack the submarines. They arrived only yesterday by special delivery."

I remained silent at this disclosure. Not so Tom.

"How exciting," he said. "Finish off under water what we failed to complete from the air."

"Exactement ça." Fearless Tom's enthusiasm almost got him the job, before he'd been asked. "Now, this is the situation. Four of our boys did how you say, 'a dummy run'? One of them died in another operation, sadly, so we are short one boy and one over of the Limpets. The boys say it can be done by swimming from a near bay and taking the bomb straight to the submarines. With a 30-minute fuse to escape before the explosion. It must be done. Dangerous but we all think we must do it."

Fearless Tom raised his hand,

"I will be your fourth boy."

The Frenchmen applauded. I was less pleased at the diversion which would delay my own plan until the sub issue was out of the way.

Tom was the hero of the moment. I hoped we would not live to regret his fearless, fearful decision.

Chapter Nineteen

With alarming rapidity, our hosts set up residence for us in Bordeaux. Their EOE contact in London had let it be known that the notorious U178 was likely to be unleashed to the oceans within 48 hours. Here was a serious debt to be repaid and its destruction was top priority.

I was allowed to accompany Tom, as long as, again, we did not live at the same location. The address sounded glamorous. He was at number 5 'Les Allées de l'Amour' and I was a few doors away at number 15. We were assured that both were safe houses. We found ourselves at the centre of the harbour low life. The bars and bistros were filled to capacity. Tom's room was on the first floor of one such establishment. Sexy, scantily-clad girls flitted around happy to do business with anyone who had a few francs to their name. We enjoyed the entertainment on offer and felt there was safety in numbers. It was as good a way as any to spend time in the stressful hours before the attack.

Opposite there stood a magnificent Basilique Church, St. Seurin, in a square of its own. In less turbulent times, I would have wished to inspect what lay beneath the huge steeples that towered skywards.

Our Resistance friends had given us some francs spending money. Tom told me the morning after that he had fallen into some innocent banter with a gorgeous French girl called Monique, who had no difficulty luring him to her room. After his allocated 20 minutes of passion, there was a knock on the door. Tom was not quite 'done'. Monique called out, "Une minute, s'il vous plaît." The waiting German soldier took her literally and checked the second hand of his watch. After 60 seconds, he tried the handle of the door and to the discomfort of all concerned, found it unlocked. He stood in the doorway just in time to see Tom 'disengage'. He cast a watchful and impatient eye as Tom pulled up his trousers and kissed the girl goodbye. Even if the German had realised they were adversaries in war, he had more important matters in mind at that moment.

The next day it was down to business.

We met our contact at the church. He led us to his parked car, already occupied by an elderly English-speaking Frenchman, who introduced himself as 'Guy'. He wore a hat, sported a greying beard and had the demeanour of a highly intelligent professor. We were soon to discover that he was a weapons expert, loyal to the Resistance, with an overload knowledge of anything explosive. The young man driving was Jean-Paul. He navigated the back streets of Bordeaux with skill and experience to eliminate any chance of hitting a road-block or similar impediment. Surprising, I thought, since he looked barely old enough to drive, let alone blow up a submarine. Tom and I sat in the back seat. Conversation was sparse, which made me feel redundant for the time being, since I had been invited to the party only as interpreter to ensure Tom followed all that was being said. My French was evidently considered adequate for this task. After a while the busy town gave way to a country lane, with the odd primitive farmhouse on either side.

After 20 minutes, we pulled up at what looked like a disused garage. Unaccustomed to any cars on its forecourt, Jean-Paul parked at the back so as to be unseen by any passing vehicles.

Before we had the chance to get out, two young men appeared from nowhere. Clearly they were colleagues of Jean-Paul, since they greeted him with great affection. Introductions were quickly made and we were soon to learn that Danny and François were to make up the raiding party with Tom and Jean-Paul. None of them looked much beyond teen-age.

We entered the musty old building for which Jean-Paul held the key. The stale arid smell of damp and neglect suggested it had not seen much human life for many years. Brushing aside cobwebs in dim lighting, we found our way to some steps that led to a dingy basement. Miraculously, electricity was available, since a light switch revealed a small room with a bench at the side and a table, which had been prepared with all the equipment that we would need for the operation. There were four rubber suits with fins on the table, four special holdall belts by their sides. On the bench were four medium sized objects that looked like gigantic beetles, since the main body had three extensions on each side that could have been their legs. Only these were made of the toughest Sheffield steel.

Guy removed his jacket and hat, ready to explain the intricacies of the gadgets that had been assembled. His handling of them indicated that he was an expert in the field of 'Limpet' mines. He rolled up his sleeves and gave us a lecture of what the various components were and how they worked. He spoke in French for the benefit of Jean-Paul, Danny and François. Then painstakingly translated every sentence into good English, so that Tom would know as much as his French colleagues. He made it clear that he had handled these weapons before. He picked one up with expertise and started to explain, first French then adequate English, so that my services were not required.

"So this, Gentlemen is the Limpet mine." He picked it up with one hand quite easily to show it was not heavy. "The body, which looks like a flask, contains four and a half pounds of explosive. It is powerful enough to blow a large hole into the hull of any ship that does not have reinforced steel, 6-8 feet below the surface." He pointed to the three extensions either side. "These are the magnets. They are the most powerful magnets ever known. They will bind the mine tight – it will need heavy machinery to remove." He handed a mine to each of the boys. "See how light it is. No no, do not worry, it will not explode... not yet. Now I show you the hollow compartments here and here." He pointed with a crooked finger. "This will reduce the buoyancy and make it easier to handle under water." He illustrated how it should be set. He suggested 20 minutes to allow the divers to escape the blast. Each one of us tested the time-fuse, setting it and then showing Guy the clock for verification. "Now let us test the strength of these tiny magnets and see how powerful they are." There was a steel jack standing in a corner, relics of when car repairs had been done in the past. "Now each of you put your Limpet on this equipment. Feel the magnets bite and then try to remove it." Tom tried and couldn't; even with two others to help, it was immovable. "Now this button withdraws the magnet." He pushed it and got a release. "But the Boches they do not know about this and in the water six foot down the pressure will not allow the magnet to withdraw."

Tom said, "Incredible little beast," he kissed it, "you're bloody well going to do the job for me tonight." The boys stayed to get the feel of it and declared themselves satisfied that they were ready. "Pas encore, mes amis," said the bi-lingual Guy. "Put on your rubber suits." We did, with difficulty. "Put on and take off several times until it becomes easier. Don't forget, you may have to do this in the car. Plus difficile," he smiled. "Now the special belt. Put it around your waist... so. The pouch holds the Limpet which gives you hands free. Please try." For thirty minutes the team got used to the feel of all the equipment while Guy looked on, pleased that his instruction had been understood and well received. He made a little speech. "Messieurs, I have the honour of instructing three Frenchman and one Englishman on how to use this British weapon. A very good blend of Anglo French cooperation." There was some muted applause. He continued, "We are working together to destroy a submarine that has sunk tens of thousands of tons of Allied shipping. Not only that, but the merciless gunning down of survivors as they cling to lifeboats in the hope of survival. Such a boat and crew deserves to be eliminated and that, mes amis, is what I hope you will achieve tonight. We are informed by our friends that that the vessel may sail in the morning. The usual time is first light, maybe 6 a.m. It is probable the shutters will be open tonight and this is our opportunity to strike. Good luck, mes amis. Vive la France... Vive l'Angleterre. We will meet here at 2100 hours for a final briefing. Bonne chance, mes amis, bonne chance."

Chapter Twenty

The night of reckoning had been planned to a strict timetable, accountable in minutes and seconds. Jean-Paul had emerged the clear leader of the operation. For his young years, he had proved himself a brilliant organiser and now calm in the execution of his plan. He spoke little English, just enough to communicate.

At 00.00 hours the two cars had moved into position in the yard outside a disused cargo warehouse. The oily waters of the River Gironde were close by. They were at Bacalon, a Bordeaux suburb, whose vast man-made deep water harbour was easily accessible to the submarines and other cargo vessels that serviced the city. The target lay one mile eastwards. The tide would favour them on the outward journey. The only signs of life were seagulls swooping down, hoping for early-rising fish. Tom was with Jean-Paul. They already wore rubber suits, covered by shirts so as not to look conspicuous for the drive.

At 00.05 the four boys emerged from the cars and synchronised watches. They helped each other with their oxygen cylinders and put the carrier belts into position. Then they gently picked up their Limpets fully charged and primed, and fitted them into the pouch. All that needed to be done was set the fuse, on reaching the target, allowing 20 minutes to clear the site. They put on goggles, flippers and finally the mouth-pieces. Mutual thumbs-up confirmed that everything was in order. At 00.15 they stood on the edge of the quay ready to take the vertical steps that took them down to the water of the vast river estuary. They carefully descended backwards and submerged the moment they hit the icy water.

The moon was hidden by low cloud causing persistent drizzle. They planned to swim in pairs, so that Tom and Jean-Paul would reach the target one minute before Danny and François. Jean-Paul carried wire-clippers, since they were anticipating a protective mesh, surrounding the base. After swimming for 15 minutes they came to it. Silent prayers that it was not linked to an alarm system, which would have signalled an immediate abort. The clippers cut a small aperture deep enough to allow the divers to pass through. There seemed to be no alarm.

After a further five minutes swimming, the outline of the massive construction that was their target came into view. They edged forward, keeping close to the seaward wall. The shutters on the first six bays were firmly in place. But as they inched slowly forward a shaft of light appeared near the end of the line. This was the news they wanted. The shutter was open and within it, hopefully the U178 exposed ready for its launch at dawn. Thumbs up again, but nerves jangled as they approached the shaft of light. Concerns that air bubbles might be spotted, that the sub might sail before they got there were ever present. The two pairs were now within 20 yards of strike. No more time for apprehension. This was the moment, the culmination of all their plans. They trod water to fix fuses so that the explosion would rip the sub apart in 23 minutes from now. That done, they were ready for the final assault. As they swam past the dividing wall, there was the beast in front of them. From 8 feet down and staring up at the bow, the vessel looked gigantic. In the underwater haze, its length could not be fully assessed. It looked evil and sinister stationary, so what it must have been like to meet in action was not a good thought.

The first pair got busy. Limpet in hand they checked again that everything was in place; then planted them fair and square on the side of the vessel, about 20 feet apart. There was relief and thumbs up as the magnets bit and held. Stage one completed now the race to get away before the explosions. The second pair was already making its mark on the sub.

On the way back they reached the wire mesh, trying to find the opening cut earlier. Frustration. They could not, either too high or too low, too east or too west, it eluded them. They wasted valuable seconds searching in vain. This was not expected; Jean-Paul still had the clippers strapped to his belt. A further incision didn't take long. Now there was despair. The second pair could not be seen. They carried under-water torches, to be used only in moments of acute emergency. This was one such. Jean-Paul flashed his torch in three ten-second bursts, by previous arrangement. No sign of the missing pair in the murky waters. Visibility was not good. More flashes with the torch. Valuable seconds lost were straining the timetable. Jean-Paul signalled Tom to start swimming away. He declined, preferring to tread water awhile. This was the most worrying moment of the entire operation. More flashes of the torch finally got a result. Relief as the two divers emerged from the gloom; they had lost their bearings looking for the opening. Now there was an extra emission of bubbles to denote heavy breathing, thumbs up with relief at finding each other.

The four divers used their flippers well to speed up the swim. At one point Jean-Paul surfaced to take bearings and found they needed to go west to reach the warehouse. The hit-or-miss navigation worked. They broke surface at the right spot, clambered up the iron steps and heaved themselves onto dry land. Stop watches were checked. The first of the explosions was due in two minutes 35 seconds.

The moment they set foot on dry land, the rubber suits, cylinders and flippers were removed at great speed and stuffed into the car boot. For a brief moment they stood shivering in their briefs, grasping to find their clothing. And then it happened at the precise moment they had calculated. Two explosions of considerable force shattered the peace of the night. Wild life took fright. Birds squawked overhead. The explosions were muffled, being 6 feet below the surface. Moments later the second pair of explosions joined the reverberations of the first. All four Limpets had done their work. No one spoke for a moment. Then mutual congratulations. The mission impossible seemed to have succeeded.

They didn't allow euphoria to delay their departure. The Germans would be out in force. Speed of escaping the area was vital. A brief 'farewell' and they were on their way. There were further explosions with a series of flashes that momentarily robbed them of night cover. They suspected that torpedoes might have blown up the sub. Now, beyond doubt, the U178 had been dealt its death blow. She might not sink, but fair revenge had been exacted. She would never kill again.

The Allied sea-faring community and the oceans at large would be a better place without her.

Chapter Twenty-One

Jean-Paul looked in the mirror with concern. There was no traffic either way, which made the motorbike, lights blazing, all the more alarming.

"Attention. En arrière," he muttered to Tom. They both drew their pistols. Jean-Paul realised he had only one option – to pull up. The German, if indeed he was one, would have to dismount and stand his bike. This would be the moment he was vulnerable. They had the split-second advantage of stopping first. Getting out quickly would give them a chance. The rider looked as though he was going to pull up behind. At the last moment, he swerved, made a large loop and sped past.

Jean-Paul knew every back-street in town.

"We take zig-zag route to town. Then leave car and walk. D'accord?"

"OK," Tom said, not a little shaken by events. He chose a route that showed Jean-Paul to be a racing driver in the making. Perhaps after the War. He was young and fearless. He headed inland at maximum speed, crunching the gears up and down to get the greatest impact from the ageing Renault. He took corners on two wheels, twisting and turning his way into the Old Town. Fortunately the roads were clear of vehicles and pedestrians.

"I zink we must leave ze car. Trop dangereux, if he was German man. Zay look for car, not persons." Jean-Paul put the sentence together with his limited English.

"What you zink?" Tom was happy to follow him, after the brilliant raid he had masterminded. However, he made the wrong decision.

"I zink we drive to l'Église St Seurin, I leave car and walk," he suggested. "I go one way, you go ze ozer." This was Resistance training. Never get caught together. It seemed a good idea at the time and Tom trusted him. Having shaken off the rider, he drove less violently, though eager to dump the car at the first opportunity.

One hundred yards from the church, a group of soldiers was constructing a road block, which could not be passed... Neither was there space or time to U-turn. A convenient curb offered the only solution. They dumped the car in it and started to walk in the opposite direction. Not far. A group of soldiers was marching towards them. No chance of separating now. They were trapped. They dodged into an open doorway leading to the stairs. It looked familiar to Tom. They took the stairs two at a time to the third floor. Jean-Paul followed, not quite sure what Tom had in mind. At least they had escaped the German soldiers, for the time being anyway.

Tom tried the door. It was locked. In a soft but plaintive voice, he called her name, "Monique... Monique." He wondered whether she might be with a client, perhaps even a German. He held his pistol at the ready, just in case. Jean-Paul understood at once.

"Ah. Une amie. Quelle chance."

Tom knocked again. "Monique. Monique," more urgently. Came the reply of someone who had been awoken sharply.

"Je dormais... je regrette. J'ai fini. Venez demain, Monsieur, s'il vous plaît." And evidently, back to sleep.

Then Monique heard the voice of a second man – a Frenchman. She was not accustomed to French clients in times of the occupation. He spoke urgently and offered her 1000 Francs. This woke Monique. No one in her whole career had ever offered her such a sum. Maybe a double-date and 1000 Francs was worth opening up for. It hadn't been a good night and she had the rent to pay next day... She put on her dressing gown, tied the belt securely and opened the door. Jean-Paul pulled a wad of dirty notes from his trouser pockets. "Les Boches sont ici. C'est possible de rester ici quelques minutes... pas longtemps?"

Even without make-up and half asleep, she still looked beautiful. It seemed a travesty to give her all that money for only sanctuary... perhaps after the Germans had gone... thoughts that Tom had to shelve with imminent danger.

She may have been a practising member of the oldest profession, but she was still a French lady, who detested German arrogance. She put the money in a vase and agreed to help her unexpected guests.

She removed her dressing gown to reveal her stunning, nubile figure, but gave the boys little chance to admire it, since she went back to bed. Tom had to smile even in adversity. Three in a bed was farcical.

Monique seemed unphased and lay in the middle, inviting the two boys to lie either side of her. They both kept their pistols to hand in case of intruders. Tom felt trapped, but pleasantly so. An hour passed. The boys were lying on their sides facing Monique. Body contact gave them ideas beyond sanctuary.

The Germans were thorough. They had found the car and discovered the rubber suits in the boot. The perpetrators of the submarine attack must be in the area. They were searching each of the houses.

Heavy jackbooted footsteps were heard coming up the stairs. Tom checked the window to see if it offered any escape. Too high. Monique ushered him into a cupboard to hide behind an assortment of clothes. Little girlie outfits, heels, net stockings, canes and whips. She couldn't hide her profession. She had him sit on the floor and covered him with garments from the rack. As she closed the cupboard door, he had disappeared from sight under a pile of her clothes. He still carried his pistol.

Monique turned to Jean-Paul.

"Alors, tu es mon mari, d'accord? Disons que nous étions ensemble toute la soirée. Viens vîte au lit." She covered him with the duvet and climbed beside him as might any husband and wife. He was ready to use the pistol that he kept in hand. They heard the sound of guttural German voices as the ground floor was ransacked. Then the first. Finally, a single soldier split from his partner to search the third floor. He did not knock and barged in.

"Qu'est-ce qui s'est passé?" Monique asked sleepily as though she had just been awoken by the intrusion.

"Wir suchen ein terrorist. Hast du jemand gesehen?"

She understood him well enough.

"Seulement mon mari. Il n'est pas un terrorist, je vous assure."

"Wollen wir mal gucken," he said to himself and tore the duvet from the bed. Jean-Paul revealed, the German left the room onto the landing,

"Hier oben. Komm' schnell Fritz."

Jean-Paul jumped out of the bed and shot the German in the back. He leant heavily on the timber frame banister which broke and he somersaulted down to the ground floor. His colleague came over to investigate. With the element of surprise in his favour, Jean-Paul shot him between the eyes. He ran out into the street, ready to shoot again if necessary. He ran into the church for refuge and hid behind a giant crucifix for cover. A group of Germans had seen his desperate bid for freedom. They followed him in. One had a megaphone and called.

"Komm' raus, Bursche." Words with a sinister echo. "Wir werden dich bald finden. Komm' raus mit Händen hoch."

Clearly they knew he was there but not where. He kept quite still. They had to find him first and the church was large. Jean-Paul could see, lying flat on his stomach, that there were four of them. They knew he was armed and were not prepared to take risks. They shouted for tear gas, which arrived painfully quickly. They fired six canisters. One rolled near to his hiding place, which would have blinded him. He broke cover, picked it up and threw it at the Germans. He shot his pistol twice as he ran to the nave seeking new cover. He could see one of the Germans hit, writhing on the floor. Another seemed to have been injured. He prayed that the House of God might come to his rescue.

The two soldiers carried machine guns. The gallant Frenchman fired his pistol hoping to take another one out, but he was no match for the machine guns which sprayed him with bullets. He lay on the marble floor, bleeding heavily from the face and chest. A noble Frenchman had died for his country in pursuit of freedom. He could be thankful not to have been taken prisoner.

Upstairs in her bedroom on the 3rd floor, Monique knelt by the cupboard, pretending to fold her clothes.

"Reste tranquille, mon ami," she said, and in English,

"They soon go away… then you come in bed with me."

Chapter Twenty-Two

It was a day to remember.

I knew the timetable by heart. I wanted to accompany them, but it was deemed unwise.

I looked at my watch throughout the day following their movements. I wondered whether Tom would still be fearless, now that the most dangerous task of his life was about to take place.

I was with them in spirit at 0015, when I knew they would be wading into the ocean. Over the next 30 minutes, I stood, I sat, I walked, I looked at my watch. I counted the seconds and pretended they were sheep. I bought myself a crepe and a drink and consumed neither. I discovered my throat was too tight to eat or drink. I went in and out of my 'digs' incessantly. My landlady, caring, overweight, Madame Castillon asked why I was so restless.

"Asseyez-vous, Monsieur, et prenez un verre avec moi," she expressed her concern.

"Merci..." I started to decline, "mais j'attends quelque chose."

End of conversation mercifully. I got up to move before any further questions were asked. With that I resumed my little walk up the road to the main square, then back round the church. I calculated that each round trip took seven minutes. I checked my watch after the second tour... by now they should have fixed the Limpets. By 0100 I should have heard the sound of the explosions, but nothing happened.

I was beginning to talk myself into failure mode. Such a mission impossible it was, so fraught with danger. Another tour, another seven minutes, half way round a further one, the moment I had been praying for, happened. Two muted explosions, followed one minute later by two further ones. All four had made it. I wanted to jump up and down, kiss or hug someone. Fortunately, no one was in sight.

A short time after, a fifth louder explosion was heard. Briefly the sky lit up as though a huge bomb had exploded. I grew worried. Four minor explosions I was expecting. But a fifth, where did that come from? Maybe it was the sub hitting back at the divers? Would that be such a large explosion? It did cross my mind that it might have been a torpedo blowing up, triggered by the Limpets. What a coup that would be. The U178 destroyed by its own torpedo. Retribution at its finest. Callously, I hoped that the crew might have been on board. I walked the distance between Tom's lodgings and mine, then round the church. Anything to keep moving. Then I saw an alarming sight. A group of German soldiers was constructing a road block fifteen yards from where I was staying. I thought it best to come off the street and stay in the room.

Shortly after, a knock on my door. A very agitated Madame Castillon stood there, her vast frame heaving with agitation.

She was already breathing heavily, which was to deteriorate.

"Monsieur, les Allemands. Ils sont en train de fouiller toutes les maisons. Ils cherchent quelqu'un, évidemment." She stopped to take a deep breath. "Je vous en prie, Monsieur. Il faut vous cacher."

I understood most of what she said, except the word 'fouiller'. I asked her what it meant. She gave me a graphic explanation of a search. The exertion left her with beads of perspiration on her face.

"Vîte, Monsieur, vîte. Venez avec moi, je vous en prie." Her short stubby legs had already taken her down the passage leading to the kitchen and a door that led to the garden. I was compelled to follow her. We headed for a shed, obviously used for storing coal. She handed me a spade and I followed her lead in digging down to reveal a manhole, which led to a cellar. By now she was sweating profusely and used the corner of her dress to wipe away the perspiration.

"C'est pas très agréable, le charbon, mais les Boches vous ne trouveraient pas ici." She beckoned me towards the manhole. "Allez vous-y, je vous en prie. Vous trouverez un petit escalier. Prenez le, pour descendre... Vîte... Vîte."

I did as she asked. The cellar was deep, dark and full of coal. The little light there disappeared when the manhole was shut. I heard her shovelling coal to conceal it. This must have continued for several minutes, to keep the German soldiers away. I imagined the state of poor Madame Castillon. Covered in perspiration and scarcely able to draw breath. Meanwhile my own predicament did nothing for my oncoming claustrophobia.

Stuck in the blackest hole without ventilation or light, trying to get comfortable on a pile of coal was far beyond the call of duty. If abandoned here, I thought to myself, for how long could I survive? If, God forbid, the rotund, perspiring Madame Castillon had a heart attack, and she looked very close, I was doomed to a dreadful death stifled by coal-dust. I moved around a little, trying to gauge the size of the cellar. It was difficult and dangerous trying to walk on coal. I decided it would be safer to crawl. My hands, face, hair and clothing were covered in the blackest coal dust. I now had a rough idea of the size of my incarcerated hell-hole. I could see a dim circle of light, which I assumed to be the manhole. I crawled towards it and stood up to see if I could touch it. Just with my fingertips. A useful exercise, I thought, to build a coal platform beneath it to see if I could achieve any leverage to escape when the crisis was over. It seemed to have several tons of coal on it and I got little if any result.

I froze in my tracks. I could hear voices above me. Madame Castillon had been commanded to show the search party around the shed. An officer ordered his men to move slabs of coal to see if a fugitive might be beneath them. But the effusive Madame Castillon had managed to put so many layers of coal above the manhole that the Germans soon lost heart.

"Scheisse," they swore, "hier kann niemand sein." They looked at their filthy hands and boots in despair, appealing to their officer to move on. He snapped his fingers at the men.

"Weiter, nächstes Haus. Los. Schnell." Rubbing their hands in an unsuccessful attempt to clean them, the soldiers left the shed. The officer turned to a still-perspiring Madame Castillon,

"Wir suchen einen Terroristen. Wenn du irgend etwas siehst, sofort telefonieren." He put his hand to his ear in the sign of a telephone. "Verstehst du?"

She hadn't understood a word but dutifully replied, "Bien sûr, mon Capitaine."

He smiled modestly at his promotion!

To my discomfort, but with intelligent discretion, Madame Castillon busied herself in the kitchen for what seemed an eternity, before coming to retrieve me. Meanwhile I was groping around in the dark and stumbled into what I believed to be a hoist. I climbed onto the metal base to see if the shaft led anywhere that I could reach. There was no daylight, nor means to activate it, so I assumed it had to be operated from above.

My efforts to escape left me breathless. Worse, I was inhaling coal dust. My ankle was throbbing and I was feeling drowsy. I decided to sit quietly and await my fate. The voice of Madame Castillon was never sweeter, as I heard her say,

"J'arrive, Monsieur. Restez tranquille. Les Boches sont partis. Une minute."

I shouted back, "Merci beaucoup." Then I heard the noise of coal being lifted manually from the area of the manhole and deposited elsewhere. Waiting so urgently for my release, each lump of coal seemed to take progressively longer to remove than the one before it. I started counting seconds in between each and she came near to a standstill after 20 lumps. I visualised the poor overweight lady sweating and breathing heavily with fatigue. Her voice sounded faint as she tried to reassure me.

"Attendez, Monsieur. Je suis..." She didn't finish the sentence. There was no further movement. I suspected the worst. I shouted up to her,

"Arrêtez, Madame. Je vais essayer."

The good lady had moved a pile. I stood on the platform I had built and heaved myself upwards with all my strength. I didn't make it first time, but the leverage had been created. Two more attempts. Gradually the manhole was easing open and with a final thrust, I felt the residue coal fall away. I finally heaved myself out of the cellar.

The luxury of air and light left me dizzy. I closed my eyes, blinked at the first sight of daylight. I had escaped death by carbon monoxide poisoning. I felt very close to it. Madame Castillon had saved my life pushing me in and again getting me out. How could I ever thank her? As my half-open eyes became accustomed to the bright light, I squinted to see her lying by the side of the manhole, still clutching a lump of coal. Her hands and face were covered in coal-dust. The sweat on her body was still warm. Her eyes were closed, her legs akimbo. I checked her pulse and heartbeat. Nothing. Her mouth was open as though gasping for air had been her last throw. I called her name and shook her face. No result. My tears made little arteries over my blackened, coal-dusted face. The body lying still and lifeless was to haunt me for many a day. A good woman had died in vain. A Patriot of France with a loathing of the Germans who had raped her country.

"Dear God," I beseeched Him, "please give me strength to find and kill the Bastard." The list of those I had to avenge had grown again.

Chapter Twenty-Three

Tom declined the offer of a sexy lie-in with Monique to his deep regret. The Germans might come back, asking questions. They had clutched Jean-Paul from under the dubious security of Monique's duvet and he didn't want to share a similar fate.

Having shifted countless pairs of shoes, he was able to stretch his legs on the hard floor-space of Monique's wardrobe. He even found some sleep, pleasantly covered by her sweaters, undies and extraneous bedwear, all enriched with the sweet smell of her perfume.

He didn't dare leave the building, since, having heard the shoot-out in the church, and, fearing the worst, he assumed the patrols were still out in force. He was dozing gently at 8.30 a.m., when the smell of coffee awoke him. Monique was walking around on tiptoe, wearing little more than a slip that barely covered her hips.

She peeped into her cupboard to check that her lodger was still there. "Oh La La," was all she said, when she saw her precious apparel used as sheets, pillows and blankets. "Monsieur désire le petit déjeuner?" she enquired sweetly.

Since he had eaten very little the past 24 hours, an irresistible suggestion.

He rose from his nocturnal retreat, stiff and aching, to sit on the bed next to the girl. To go with the coffee, she had some of yesterday's croissants left, stale but edible. In less troubled times, it would have been a romantic breakfast in the company of a beautiful girl, to be followed by sex and sleep. But now, Tom's main preoccupation was escape. Destination: 12 Place Maritime which was a safe house, their pre-arranged rendezvous.

He asked her advice. She lit her first Gauloise of the day and thought through an idea. Far-fetched, Tom thought, but fearless as ever, he felt it was his best option.

She showed him the accommodation on the landing outside the flat, which was to play a vital role. There was a musty little-used broom cupboard aside a small toilet, with bidet. They talked about the plan at length in a mixture of French and English. She had acquired a working knowledge of most European languages. "Good enough at least to give them prices," she quipped.

She produced a board, written in beautiful graphic print, which gave the client some important instructions. One side in German, the other English. When Tom read the English version, his laughter was so noisy, she put her hand over his mouth until he got control. It was a lighter moment in a day that promised to be heavy.

When he had calmed down, he asked if she had produced the magnificent graphics. "A work of art," he said. She told him half her life story; of how she had been reading Art at university, when the war interrupted her studies. Worse, her father had died defending the Maginot Line, albeit unsuccessfully. So she was left unfunded, unloved and homeless. "Et violà," she concluded philosophically, "c'est ma vie maintenant et il faut continuer jusqu'à la fin de la guerre."

Tom kissed her on hearing the story of how she had fallen on hard times. What a lovely girl, he thought. A pro, with a heart and obvious talent. She put a hand on her thigh as though to reciprocate sympathy. "You want quickie?" A statement rather than a question because Tom had already unzipped. "On ze house," she joked, perhaps in memory of the 1000 Francs that Jean-Paul had given her, with very little service provided other than sanctuary. He knew he should have declined, but there she was half-naked, looking irresistible.

The 'quickie' was anything but. Tom saw no reason to rush. He was taking his pleasure at leisure, thinking it might be his last.

Still no sign of the enemy, they inspected the broom cupboard and rearranged contents to allow for a stool with space to sit. The door had a key, but he would need to keep it ajar to watch the traffic and give him air. Monique, meanwhile, gave her shattered wardrobe some much needed attention and selected her outfit for the day. Minutes later she appeared on the landing wearing a provocative red dress that would drop to the ground at the release of a button. Tom had reason to believe that she wore nothing beneath and her heels gave extra height. She had applied make-up and was ready for her first client, looking ravishing. Tom looked at the finished product in admiration. Glamorous beyond belief and a genuinely nice person. He kissed her ruby red lips, even at the risk of smudging.

"Monique," Tom declared lovingly. "Après la guerre – I will come and find you and marry you. I swear it."

She laughed. "Tu es 'méchant, toi, vraiment 'méchant." She pushed him away, flattered nonetheless. They laughed as though they didn't have a care in the world.

Tom then began his lonely vigil in the cupboard room.

After an hour's inactivity, he had thoughts of abandoning his plan and making a run for it. Then he recalled Jean-Paul's ill-fated dash and decided against it. By lunch-time there were no takers. His little space was uncomfortable and air-less. He held the door open, as Monique appeared, locked the door behind her, and pinned a notice on the door saying 'Closed for lunch. Back in 10 minutes'.

"Ça va?" she whispered on the way out.

"Horrible."

"Soit patient. L'après-midi il y aura du monde."

"J'espère."

"Tu veux manger quelque chose. Un sandwich peut'être?"

"Very good." He kissed her.

"Stupide." She pushed him away playfully, implying no more 'freebies'.

She came back ten minutes later with a ham sandwich and a watery drink of orange juice. They stood on the landing, chatting and eating together, as if they were lovers. If a client approached there would be three flights of stairs to get into position.

It happened quite quickly. A young German subaltern crept tentatively, noiselessly up the stairs, so quietly they were almost caught unawares. They managed to get into position just in time. Tom peeped through a crack in the door, so that he could watch unseen. The officer was in full uniform. When he got to the top floor, he saw Monique's name on the door. He hesitated nervously, not sure whether to knock or flee. He removed his cap and combed his hair. Then took the plunge and knocked politely.

"Guten Tag, mein Herr," Monique said in passable German. "Kommen Sie herein."

"Danke schön," he said nervously, looking her over before committing himself.

Sensing his hesitation, she offered him a drink.

"Wünschen Sie etwas zu trinken?" She smiled invitingly. "Ich habe Apfelsaft, Wasser oder schnapps." That seemed to break the ice. He entered. Monique locked the door behind him.

"Schnapps bitte. Danke vielmals," he was relieved to be in the company of such a beautiful mistress.

"Cigarette?"

"Danke schön."

They lit up together and drank schnapps. She knew her trade well. If a client was young and nervous, she knew how to get him relaxed.

"Ich heisse Monique."

"Und ich bin Otto."

"Herr Otto," she said respectfully, "Sie wollen zwangzig Minuten mit mir verbringen?"

"Etwas länger, wenn möglich."

"20 Minuten ist 100 Francs, oder mehr, wenn länger. Was wünschen Sie… Herr Otto, etwas Besonderes?"

He had something special in mind, but was clearly too embarrassed to say what. This was the moment Monique showed her board, the same that Tom had found so hilariously funny. He read it first in English and then turned it over to read the German translation:

PLEASE UNDRESS IN THE BATHROOM NEXT DOOR THEN WEAR DRESSING GOWN PROVIDED. IF YOU REQUIRE SOIXANTE-NEUF (69), PLEASE USE BIDET AND WASH. THOROUGHLY.

He smiled on full understanding in his own language.

"Jawohl. Bitte." Having made his decision, he stubbed out the cigarette and swallowed the Schnapps in a single gulp.

"Also, das macht 200 Franken für 30 Minuten."

"Sehr anständig," he said pulling out his wallet and handing her the money. She placed it in her vase.

Tom had been listening to the conversation and had to move quickly into his hiding place as the door was unlocked and the young officer moved into the bathroom. He must have used the bidet for over five minutes, obviously observing the instruction to 'wash thoroughly'. He finally emerged, wearing a blue towelling gown, clutching his wallet, which he placed in one of the large pockets. He combed his hair again to ensure it was perfect and knocked the door. This was the moment Tom had to move and quickly. He had 30 minutes to make his escape. Otto had folded his uniform neatly into a little square pile on the only chair in the room. In seconds Tom had the brown shirt and battledress jacket on his shoulders. Seconds more for the trousers and boots. The cap took a little longer and needed a mirror to check. The uniform fitted him well. He rolled up his own clothes into a ball and put them into a bag, Monique had provided. Then he was ready. If the Germans were watching the building, they would have noted Otto's entrance and his exit should not arouse suspicion.

Casually Tom sauntered onto the road as though he hadn't a care in the world. He knew the way to Place Maritime and headed in that direction. He saw some patrol cars, but they paid no attention. He wanted to put as much distance between himself and Monique as possible without seeming to be in a hurry. The walk was probably two kilometres. He looked around constantly to check if he was being followed. He quickened his pace when no one appeared in sight. He looked at his watch and worried about Monique. She was left holding the baby. Would they hold her responsible for the stolen uniform and poor Otto, how would he cope. With acute embarrassment for sure. Well, thought Tom, the fellow had the benefit of 30 minutes with the best bird in town and all such pleasures carried their penalty. Place Maritime came into view...

Chapter Twenty-Four

One thing was certain; I couldn't leave poor Madame Castillon in a coal shed covered in thick black dust. She had saved me twice and the least I could do was to clean her up before she met her maker. It was a grisly job. First I had to get her out of the shed and on to the grass. At an estimated twenty stone, I could not lift her. I took her by the armpits and dragged her out on her heels. Then I left her on a grassy patch, while I went into the house to find detergent, towels, sheets and a bucket.

Whilst upstairs, I glanced out of the window to be reminded of my predicament. A German solider was guarding the front entrance. He was obviously relaxed, enjoying a smoke, left behind by the main search party to keep the building under surveillance. I moved around cautiously, keeping my distance from the window.

I had no experience in cleaning up corpses. Rigour mortis had already started to set in. The podgy fingers had stiffened as I tried to dip them into the water bucket. Very soon it was black and I returned to the house to refill it. A procedure I had to repeat many times. I used a towel to dab her face. The flesh was tightening. She was wearing ankle socks originally white, now turned black. I removed them releasing a shower of coal-dust. Her bare legs were stiff and bent, but quite easy to clean. The towels were now filthy and sodden. More were needed to finish the job. Another visit to the house. I noticed the sentry still there, leaning against the gate. I prayed he would have no inclination to rest his weary bones inside the house.

I was so preoccupied with cleaning up Madame Castillon, that I hadn't given much thought to my own state of filth and how I was ever going to escape, particularly with the guard in the front. Dawn was breaking. I would clearly have to hang around until nightfall, hoping that by then the surveillance would be called off. Meanwhile I had another one hour's cleaning to do on Madame Castillon at which point she was as clean as she was going to get. I dragged her away to a dust-free zone and rolled her onto a white sheet that I had spread on the ground. She was lying on her back, I gently rested her head on a pillow, managed to fold her stiffened hands so they rested on her stomach. I had another sheet to cover her. Having done as much for her as I was able, I knelt in prayer. "Dear God, Look after this lovely lady, who saved my life in the name of France. A good person who did not deserve to die." That was as much of a burial as she was going to get from me. I had thought of digging a grave, but that was for the next of kin, whom maybe I should contact.

I noticed a lot of papers strewn over a desk upstairs, but concluded it might provoke questions that I would not wish to answer. My final task was to cover the manhole, so that no one would realise the drama that had taken place around it.

That done, I considered my debt to the formidable Madame Castillon repaid. Now I needed to look after myself. I was sweating profusely, black coal-dusty sweat that made me feel even more wretched. My hair, face, hands, legs and clothes were covered in it. I had noticed a stained old-fashioned bathtub upstairs and considered this my best and only option. I ran it full and moments of bliss later, I sank into its cleansing waters. They were jet black within seconds. Luckily there was a bar of carbolic soap to hand, which helped to restore some clear white skin. I was ready to step out of the thick grimy water. I watched it gurgle, trying to escape down the plug hole. After a moment it clogged, refusing to drain further. I couldn't deal with that as well as myself, so let it be for the next occupant. A towel to dry me absorbed more residue dust and got thrown into the filthy water.

I searched the cupboards to see if I could find any clothes. I found a wardrobe which contained men's wear. I held a pair of trousers up against me. They were enormous. Obviously, if they belonged to Mr Castillon, he was of fair size and I had to discard them. At that point a terrible thought crossed my mind. What if he were to walk in, find me in his house and a dead wife outside. It made me decide very quickly to repossess my original clothes and live within their filthy state. Putting them back on was a gruesome experience. But the thought of having to deal with Mr Castillon was even worse. Getting out of the house was my top priority. I glanced out of the window to check whether the sentry was still there. Alarmingly, yes; now chatting to a young lady in pigtails. The window was open; I could overhear their conversation.

"Bonjour," she said in a child-like voice. The solider looked her over, not particularly wanting to converse with her.

"J'aimerais voir ma grand-mère," she said unperturbed by his disinterest.

"Nein, Nein. Nicht erlaubt." He stood between her and the garden gate.

"Pourqoi pas?" the baby voice continued. "C'est son anniversaire." The solider showed no sign of comprehension. The girl knew a little German. "Ihr Geburtstag heute." She carried flowers and showed him. "Blumen für ihr Geburstag… Bitte… Bitte." She picked up each word slowly as she learnt from school studies. The soldier was unmoved.

"Niemand rein, niemand raus," he said firmly. I was relieved to hear it. The thought of having to deal with the young lady and explain to her how her grandmother had died was abhorrent.

But she didn't give up easily. She was going to see her grandmother on her birthday come what may. She had already acquired the skill of turning a 'no' into a 'yes'. She pulled two lollypops from her jacket pocket and unashamedly offered him one. He had to smile at her blatant bribery. It reminded him of his little sister, aged 10, at home in Frankfurt many miles away. She would nag until she got her way. Grudgingly he took the lollipop. It helped pass away the last minutes of his shift. He removed the wrapping paper and they stood together sucking them almost as friends.

She tried again, begged for only five minutes. He softened. He could never say 'no' to his little sister. She always got her own way in the end. 'What harm could it do?' he thought, 'a young kid visiting her granny on her birthday. It had been a long shift, he was tired and she was sweet.'

"Also, fünf Minuten, nicht länger, verstehst du? Also, mach' schnell."

"Danke, danke," she kissed him on the cheek. Now his guard was really down. Could I get to the front door before she did? I remembered seeing a heavy bolt which needed to be secured, just in case she had a key. And if she knocked, I wouldn't answer and she surely would go away. She knew her way around the house and went straight to the back, where the door stood wide open. She stood still as we came face to face. She said only two words, but they were in English. "You Peter?" I was too stunned to reply, wondering whether I should do so in French, just in case it was a trap. No need. With distinct urgency she added, "I am Resistance, my name is Suzanne. Come quick now very quick. We go out the back way." The little girly voice had disappeared. She had aged a good few years. No time to question her credentials. I followed her blindly. I had nothing to lose and escape from the sentry my reward. He was still sucking the lollipop, blissfully unaware that the 'little girl' and I were on our way out. As we passed the body near the coal shed, I stopped. The girl still carried the bunch of flowers. I took them from her and placed them on the white sheet... I bowed my head in reverence.

"Some flowers for you Madam Castillon. I thank you."

The girl didn't allow me to say any more. She grabbed my arm and pulled me away. "No time. Vîte vîte... A moment and the Germans will come looking." Now she looked very grown up. We helped each other over a high fence that separated the back garden from an overgrown pathway. I wanted to run down it. She wouldn't let me and held me back. "Resistance training," she said. Five minutes brisk walk took us to a minor road. We looked left and right cautiously, making sure we had not been followed. There was an old Peugeot car parked on the kerb, 100 yards away, its engine running. The moment we appeared, the car drove towards us. The driver was François, one of the successful divers. We stopped only long enough to shake hands and a quick embrace. Then we all piled into the car and sped away at high speed...

Chapter Twenty-Five

"That was brilliant, absolutely brilliant. I thank you. Vive la Résistance."

I spread myself over the back seat, so that I could be out of sight if required. My clothes were depositing piles of coal-dust in the process. I apologised with explanation.

François was driving at reckless speed over the bumpy road. To make it worse, he had only one hand on the wheel. The other was alternating gear change with fondling Suzanne. We stopped at a level crossing to allow a goods train to trundle past. François took the opportunity to kiss her passionately.

"Je t'adore Chérie," I heard him say.

"Moi aussi," she replied.

By now she had removed the pink ribbons and allowed the bunches to free-fall on her shoulders. She applied lipstick and looked her age – 18 as she told me.

"What a beautiful transformation," I complimented her.

"I can do any age from 14 – 40 in French, English or German."

"Incroyable."

I saw her laugh for the first time. She had a beautiful smile and very white teeth. There were so many questions I needed to ask.

"Do either of you know what happened to Tom?" No, they did not.

"Have you seen or heard from Jean-Paul?" No, they had not.

"There was shooting in the church. Who was shooting at whom?" They had no idea.

"Did they get the U178?" London was very pleased.

"I should think London was pleased. Must have been one of the most daring raids of the War. And if U178 was destroyed, there should be decorations for all concerned."

"That would be very nice indeed. Thank you London," François said with some sarcasm.

"Where are we going now?" Back to base.

"Where is base?" He would not say. His attitude was very 'Resistance'. Give nothing away. It might come back to haunt you. However he did admit that there was a long drive ahead, since his instructions were to go the long way round, to throw off the 'chasers' that might turn up en route. He gave me a clue.

"We go south before we go east. We say, 'au revoir' to Suzanne at St Émillion."

I came to the conclusion that any further dialogue with François was useless. One hour later, I saw a signpost that read: 'St Émillion 12 Kilometres'. I was informed by Suzanne that she lived in a village that was renowned for its fine wine.

"In peacetime," she boasted, "it is full of tourists, all tasting the latest blends. You wish to have a bottle and maybe take it with you?"

"That would be a very nice souvenir."

François knew exactly where to take her. Two lefts and a right and we stood outside a pretty house with a thatched roof and wild roses, growing on the outside walls. They both went in, leaving me to contemplate where I would end up and when. An hour passed. I could only imagine that they were making love. Finally Suzanne appeared with a bottle.

"Chablis 1924, a very good year." I thanked her for the thought. The lipstick had worn off and she looked flustered, confirmation that my theory was correct.

"Sorry we were so long. I had to give my parents the news," she lied.

We still had a long journey ahead. I hugged Suzanne and thanked her again for her brilliant performance. "You surely saved my life. I hope to meet you in better times."

"That would be very nice. Alors, bonne chance."

Her farewell with François took much longer. I sat in the back of the car and waited patiently while the lovers fondled and kissed each other ad nauseam.

St Émillion was not far behind us, when the accident happened.

François was driving in his usual one-hand-on-the-wheel style, travelling too fast for an emergency stop, when a black and white Collie dog came from nowhere and sauntered across the road. A belated screech of brakes and a violent swerve saved the dog, but crashed the car into another, parked outside a farmhouse.

The impact shattered the windscreen. François was oozing blood from flying glass. I had been flung to the floor of the back and thought it prudent to stay there momentarily out of sight.

For seconds, we were too stunned to move anyway. Then François staggered out to survey the damage to both cars. Ours was hissing steam from a shattered radiator and the buckled engine suggested a write-off. The other had fared as badly with a gaping hole in its side and doors hanging by their hinges. The dog, unconcerned that he was the cause of the mayhem, stood barking in the road. The farmer, brandishing a shotgun, stormed from the house, followed closely by his wife. He was shouting abuse, as only the French can, on seeing the state of his precious car. His wife took pity on the unfortunate François, now covered in blood and limping badly. His arms around her shoulder for support, she led him into the farmhouse.

"Je vais telephoner à l'Hôpital," she said.

"Et moi à la Gendarmerie," he replied angrily. They went into the house.

It was not advisable for an English pilot on the run in occupied France to get caught up in a police investigation. Quietly I opened the back door and crawled out, leaving it open in case its closure might bring out the irate farmer. My limbs seemed to be intact. The only witness to my escape was the Collie dog, wagging his tail, bewildered by the commotion.

125

I guessed that St Émillion was about five kilometres down a straight road. It turned out to be much further and took me about one and a half hours' brisk walk. A few cars passed by, but none was interested in the solitary walker, on an otherwise deserted road. I thought about, but decided against, thumbing a lift. It could have meant questions in a foreign language that I wouldn't have wished to answer.

I was heading for Suzanne's house, if only I could find it. Vaguely I remembered two lefts and a right off the main road, but from where? I walked through the quaint old town to approach it from the same direction. In less stressful times I would have liked to have stopped at the countless wine parlours that stood side by side inviting free tastings. They were mostly as built centuries ago, but a few less attractive ones had embraced modernity. Old folk were sitting outside, drinking in the morning sunshine. Possibly discussing the raging War and whether the Nazi occupation would infiltrate the vineyards producing the world's finest wines.

I think I had found my first left turning. It looked familiar. A second left and now a right, my destination stood in front of me. Still in my dusty, blackened clothes, now tired and hungry, I must have looked a bedraggled figure as I knocked on the door. I said a little prayer that Suzanne would open it. She did. Of course she was surprised to see me alone. She looked over my shoulder to see if François and the car had pulled up elsewhere. The pretty smile on her face turned to distress on hearing what had happened.

"Was he badly hurt?"

"There was blood on his face and he was limping. The car looked worse."

"Zut, alors, I must find him. There is only one little hospital in town. He will be there. Maybe under a different name. Il faut faire attention."

"Shall I come with you?" She looked me all over and decided it would not be a good idea.

"No, no, I will take my bicycle. It is the easiest way. You stay here and rest. You will be safe. Make yourself at home." She showed me round. In the kitchen, there stood a half-eaten chicken on a plate surrounded by slices of farm bread.

"You must be hungry. Please take it and wine from the cupboard."

"Thank you. I am very hungry indeed, especially after the long walk."

"And thirsty too, I am sure."

"Is there any chance you could lend me some trousers and a shirt? I will wash, iron and return after the War."

She smiled that lovely warm smile. "François has his clothes upstairs. Take whatever you want. You are the same size. They will fit you. And if you wish to shave, his razor is in the bathroom."

"How can I ever thank you?"

"Pas de quoi. C'est normale." She gave me a little kiss on the cheek.

"Au revoir. À bientôt." There was a rusty old bike standing in the hallway. She manoeuvred it out of the house, while I held the door open. In a moment she was on it and away. She waved as she went.

Chapter Twenty-Six

I was looking forward to so many good things; it was difficult to decide which to do first.

I took a leg of chicken and 'defleshed' it on the way upstairs.

My heart raced when I saw a shower cubicle complete with shampoo and various body lotions. In the bedroom, men's clothing from which I earmarked trousers, knit shirt, shoes and socks. "Thanks François," I mimed. "You've saved my life." Irritable and cocky that he was, I couldn't imagine he would approve. I removed my clothes, now stiff with coagulated coal-dust and took great pleasure in rolling them into a bundle for disposal. My body was black again, my hair, thick with soot, clogged to the scalp.

The flow of water from the rose was no more than a trickle, but enough, eventually, to clean me up. I wrapped a towel around my waist and luxuriated in the feeling of being dust-free. Even though my nostrils were now clean, the scent of coal remained, perhaps to be dispelled by a drop of wine shortly. The mess in the shower cubicle washed away quite easily and I used my sodden towel to wipe it down.

I felt a new man in François's cords and knit top, which fitted me well enough. I found a silky scarf which I put around my neck French style. Thank you François. I was ready to confront the remains of the chicken and found some French mayonnaise to spice it up. The bottle of wine Suzanne had offered me stood on the table, already emptier by two glasses.

My bodily requirements had been met in full. How could I repay the generosity of my host? I had some francs left and placed them on the table with a note expressing my gratitude, saying it was not nearly enough but all I had.

Now there was nothing to do but wait. I settled in an armchair and must have slept for some hours, since when a noise in the hallway awoke me, it was already dusk. Suzanne was wheeling her bicycle back into the house. I stood far too quickly, trying to conceal that I had been sleeping so heavily for so long. My sleepy eyes must have given me away.

"I have awoken you," she said sweetly. "I am so sorry. You deserve sleep."

I mumbled an apology. "Did you find him?"

"I did. He will be OK. His face has stitches and his leg will go into plaster. He will stay in hospital for two days, they think. The car cannot be driven again and the farmer will claim damages. Maybe the Resistance will pay, maybe not." She shrugged her shoulders as though to say, 'What will be, will be.'

"How terrible," I replied. "The War is bad enough… and now this."

"All part of the same problem, n'est-ce pas? He was very worried about you and whether you got away. I told him you were safe with me."

"Look, I feel very guilty. I have eaten your food, drunk your wine, used your shower and now I wear his clothes…"

"…and you look very handsome in them too. French style…"

I hadn't finished… "You have saved me twice, how can I repay you? I have a little money left and it is here…"

She stopped me there. "Enough. Enough. Do not talk of money, it is of no consequence. We are brothers in arms. We fight the same enemy. We help each other whenever it is necessary with one aim and one aim only – to beat the Boches. To get a free France again. Please, je vous en prie, do not leave money. That is an insult to our cause. It is my pleasure to give you the simple things that me and my house can offer. It requires no payment."

It was an eloquent appraisal, stated with charm and dignity. I thanked her again for her hospitality.

"Now I have to ring them to ask instructions." She spoke in French for some minutes on the telephone. The outcome, she told me, was that we would meet Raoul the next morning at 10 a.m. outside Café de la Paix. "You will be obliged to spend the night here. I hope you will be comfortable."

I wondered how and where she could accommodate me, since I knew there wasn't a second bedroom upstairs. I could see my night's rest being taken in the armchair on which I had slept before.

"Come with me, Peter, I will show you the wine cellar. You will be impressed."

"Rather not. I have developed a phobia of cellars."

"What means this word 'phobia'? I have not heard it before."

"Phobia is Greek for fear."

"Oh dear. I do not speak any Greek."

I elaborated on the horror of my incarceration in two different cellars.

"Not nice," she flashed me that gorgeous smile, "but this one is different. Very safe, I promise you."

She took me by the hand and led me downstairs. This cellar was civilised. Cool but not freezing, with rows of pigeon-holes, each containing a cherished bottle, beautifully labelled and corked.

"This is my father's little hobby. He is from the region and owns a vineyard. He now collects rare wines. He says they will be worth a lot of money in the years to come. Now we choose one for dinner tonight." She pulled one out at random and read from the label, "'Château Mouton-Rothschild', a good name to start with or do you fancy this one?" She pulled out another. "This is 'Château Montrose, 2eme Cru, Grande Classe St Estèphe', a vintage red wine with delicious flavour. Which you prefer with tomato omelette I will cook for us later."

I knew nothing about precious wines, but said the one with the long title sounded delicious. She put the other back in its hole. I had already consumed a bottle with the chicken lunch and was uneasy about more. I didn't like to say so for fear of offending her.

The contents of this Aladdin's cave for the serious consumer, which I certainly was not, was spectacular.

"Doesn't your father get upset when you raid his cellar?"

"On the contrary, he loves it, loves to see his choice enjoyed. Gives him a chance to bring in new wine."

"And the Germans – what happens if they find it?"

"If they find it, we are all 'foutu'."

While Suzanne cooked dinner, I twiddled some knobs on the wireless and found the BBC News. The Russians had won an heroic battle at Stalingrad. The Nazi divisions were in full retreat. Montgomery's campaign in the Middle East was coming to fruition. American forces were building up in England ready for the second front. Lancasters were pounding German cities by night and Flying Fortresses by day. I reported the good news to Suzanne.

"That is all BBC propaganda. I see no signs of the second front. That is the only news I want to hear about – when, when, when – we need it badly. We French, we are tired now and want our country back."

I reassured her. "Be patient. It will come, I promise."

She shrugged her shoulders. "Sooner rather than later."

The tomato omelette was spicy. I felt privileged to be her companion at table. The accompanying red wine was too sweet and sickly for my pallet. "Délicieux," I lied, but was obliged to drink three glasses so as not to offend her. I helped clear the dishes. She looked very attractive as she moved around the kitchen.

"I'm sorry, we have no sweet."

I assured her I had eaten and drunk too much already.

"Will you have some coffee?" she enquired.

"That would be nice, thank you."

I moved to my armchair to consume my nightcap and prepare for the night. I removed my shoes and rested my feet on the chair. She observed that I was settling down.

"Alors, I cannot allow my guest in my house to spend the night on a chair. C'est interdit… not allowed. Pas du tout. You come and sleep in my bed. It is large enough for two. You one side

131

and me the other." She made a little sign with her hands to illustrate we could sleep in the same bed without touching one another.

"That's very kind of you," I said, a little embarrassed, "but I would not wish you to be disturbed in any way."

"It will be a pleasure," she said smiling broadly. I wondered if it was wise, but the commitment was already there.

The magnetism between two semi-naked bodies is irresistible. The wine played its part, I will admit. We were both more than a little drunk. Restlessly I turned to face her. She did the same. Clearly the bed was not wide enough to keep us apart. First touch was like a mini-explosion inside me. Neither of us spoke. Our lips met. Hot searching kisses. Our hands had free access to each other's bodies. I was painfully, yet deliciously aware that I was about to make love. To take another man's girl to which I had no entitlement. At that moment, to my regret, I had no qualms. On the contrary, it stimulated my eroticism. I steam-rollered my emotions. Nor was Suzanne a reluctant participant to her infidelity. The kissing became more passionate, the breathing heavy. She played a dominant role in the act of physical exploration. I was happy to leave the initiative to her. She was astride me, teasing me with kisses that were available one moment, withdrawn the next. We lay together still... silent. I tried to hold her body still to prolong the act. She would not have it. The premature conclusion of our coitus was inevitable. We lay together still silent. It was a strange moment to be reminded of François. He had said, "Je t'aime Chérie." She had replied, "Moi aussi." And now me as well. Was it lust or love?

I said to her, "You are a fabulous girl. Sex has never been more exciting."

She said to me, "And you Monsieur Peter are an English pig, making love to another man's woman." I could see her smiling even in the dark.

"Do you have any regrets?" I said, "à la Piaf?" Thankfully she did not burst into song.

"You know, Peter, we live on the edge. Any day can be our last. We have to take our pleasures when they come. Tomorrow we may not be able to any more."

It was a philosophic answer and removed any pangs of conscience I may have felt. I kissed her on the lips before she could elaborate on the subject. We slept, but not for long. The magnetism worked again, this time for much longer. "Who needs sleep when you can make love," were her last words that night.

"Vive l'amour," were mine.

We slept soundly before stirring to check our watches. It was 9.30 a.m. We had to move fast to make our appointment.

Chapter Twenty-Seven

We were ten minutes late and for reasons of security Raoul drove around the block, rather than be seen parked outside. We decided it would be less conspicuous inside the café than standing outside it. Besides, there had been no time for 'le petit déjenuer'. We were both dying for coffee.

The café was full, but a four-seat table was vacated and we took it. Fortunately it was by the window and we could watch out for Raoul's arrival. We ordered coffee au lait and croissants.

German military was a rarity at St Émillion, particularly at 10.15 a.m. When two German officers entered the café, all eyes were on them. The hubbub of café talk subsided. Only background music and the occasional hiss of the coffee machine was audible. The officers looked around. The only available seats were at our tale. "Act naturally," Suzanne whispered as they edged in our direction. "Let me do the talking." I felt her moving into actress mode.

They enquired politely in poor but understandable French, "Vous permettez?"

Suzanne seemed excited by the notion. "Bien sûr," she said, moving her chair sideways to allow them more space. "Nous sommes en train de partir."

The Germans seemed keen to prolong our stay, if only to practise their French.

"C'est très beau ici," said one settling down.

"Ah oui."

"Et le vin est bon?"

"Il faut goûter tout ce qu'il y a."

"Un peu trop tôt maintenant," he said glancing at his watch, smiling.

"Yous parlez très bien le Français."

"J'apprends. Un peitit peu chaque jour. Vous êtes d'ici? Mademoiselle?" he asked inquisitively.

"Oui, toute ma vie. Née ici et probablement je mourirai ici." They all laughed.

"Vous êtes très jeune... et très belle aussi," he complimented her.

"Merci."

How long could this small talk continue without my participation? The officers chatted amongst themselves in German and of course I understood every word. They were suspicious of my identity, having taken no part in the dialogue. If I spoke in broken French, they would ask questions. Better to speak in poor German with a French accent. After all, there is no reason why I should not have picked up a little of their language.

"Sehr guten café hier," I contributed to the conversation with a very strong accent. "Wir kommen jeden Morgen."

"Jawohl. Also, Sie sprechen Deutsch."

"Ich habe etwas gelernt in der Schule."

"Bald wird hier mehr Deutsch gesprochen als Französich. Der Führer hat grosse Pläne, Frankreich zu annexieren. Dass wir ein Volk werden, mit nur einer Sprache."

"Sehr schön," I said politely, thinking the French would resist to the last man before losing their language to the Germans.

We could see Raoul had pulled up outside, meanwhile, and he could observe our predicament through the window. He thought it prudent to drive 100 yards down the road and wait there while we extricated ourselves from this sticky situation. "Alors, au travail," she said to the Germans.

"Auf wiedersehen," I added. The Germans rose, politeness itself.

We ambled nonchalantly to the car, aware that the Germans could watch us part of the way. Raoul greeted us angrily, furious that our late arrival had created this dangerous situation. He sped off at high speed in his borrowed Mercedes.

In the café, the senior of the two Germans asked the patron if he might use the phone for an important call, while the junior went outside just in time to see the car disappear.

Suzanne sat in the front passenger seat and I strained to overhear their conversation from behind. She explained what had happened.

Raoul did not want to make a detour to drop Suzanne off. He knew how the Germans worked. She could be picked up at any time. He accelerated on the long straight road out of town, frequently glancing in his mirror if there was any sign of a tail. He was on the road to Bergerac, when a solitary motorbike appeared. He slowed down – so did the rider. He picked up speed, the bike was still there keeping pace, equidistantly. The cat and mouse game continued for a few miles. We turned off the main road; the bike stayed with us. Raoul was watching his mirror all the time. He asked me whether I could ride a bike. I told him I had once before, but couldn't remember too much about it. In a low voice, he said to Suzanne that we had no option but to take him out. He held his pistol at the ready. He allowed the car to freewheel to a stand-still. He signalled with his hand that he was stopping, implying he had run out of fuel. By arrangement Suzanne got out of the car to wave him down, thereby to show that this was no more than a family outing. The road was free of traffic. Encouraged by Suzanne's appearance and her frantic gesticulations, the biker pulled up behind us. Raoul stayed in his seat, opened his window and concealed the pistol beneath a newspaper. The biker dismounted and stood up the machine. Suzanne played her lady-in-distress role to perfection. She assailed the biker with a torrent of non-stop French dialogue, which she knew would not be understood. Its gist, clearly, that they had broken down and were appealing for his help. Reluctantly, he walked towards the car to see if the driver could offer a more rational and slower spoken explanation of the dilemma. But first he had to make sure they were 'bona fide'. He approached the driver's open window.

"Ausweis, bitte. Ihre Papiere," he demanded.

They were his last and only words. Raoul went through the motion of finding the documents. The German may have realised he was vulnerable. Too late he attempted to pull his pistol from its holster. Raoul shot him twice between the eyes. He fell by the side of the car spurting blood. Suzanne covered her eyes. The sight was gruesome. He may have been a hated Hun, but she couldn't cope with violence at such close quarters.

Raoul and I lifted the bleeding body by its arms and legs and bundled it into the boot of the car. The whole operation took no more than 45 seconds. Time was of the essence, fearing there might be a follow-up rider or patrol car.

I sat astride the bike, trying to work out how to start it. I had very little experience. Raoul showed me how. The engine roared. The accelerator, the brake? Where were they? Driving the machine fast would be hazardous, if not dangerous.

I was relieved when Raoul made the decision. "You take the car and follow me." I could do anything on four wheels. Raoul was astride the bike in a moment and revved the engine to a crescendo and led the way at a steady 80 mph. I had to drive the Mercedes at high speed to keep up. Raoul seemed to know where he was going. He left the high road to Bergerac to avoid the town. There was safety in detour. Now the road was even narrower, bumpily turning and twisting at will. At one point he needed to steady the machine, his feet touching the ground. Had it been me, I would have been lost. Now he raced ahead again as the road straightened. Avoiding Bergerac was a wise move. As well as making pursuit impossible, the detour presented us with a deserted route, free of cars and pedestrians. I clutched the wheel firmly with both hands as the bike clocked up 100 mph on a straight road. I struggled to keep up with it.

"Thank God Raoul took the bike," I muttered to Suzanne. "I could never have ridden it like that." She agreed.

"It's hard enough to keep up with him in the car."

"You're doing OK. N'inquiète pas," she encouraged me.

"I pray we don't meet any Germans."

"Raoul knows the roads. He will keep well away from any busy places."

I looked at my watch. The wild chase had taken 90 minutes so far and we were back to negotiating country lanes. I checked the petrol gauge. It was getting close to zero.

"We haven't much fuel left," I warned.

"I think we're getting close. I see some familiar buildings."

"I would say enough fuel for ten minutes."

"The detour takes a long time, but it's safer."

"Agreed."

"I worry about the poor man in the back. Will he be OK?"

"He's a good Nazi. A dead one. Don't worry about him now – Better him than us!"

"The boot will be a bloodbath. Who will clear it up?"

"Don't worry. Raoul will know what to do."

I saw a signpost to Monflanquin. I recognised the name. This time we were approaching it from the east. We turned right up a bumpy stony drive arrowed to 'Calviac'. I had walked the drive too many times on our last visit, not to recognise it at once. Raoul and I instinctively checked mirrors to ensure there was no witness as we took the turning. We pulled up outside the small deserted church. After he put the bike on its stand, I embraced him.

"Brilliant. You should be a professional biker after the war."

"I used to be," he smiled. "But today it was more serious, n'est-ce pas! Now we have work to do. Bury the body, undress him for the uniform, hide the bike, and clean the boot."

I didn't realise at the time that he was already planning the next stage of my journey to Berlin.

The church door opened. A moment in my life that I will never forget.

He looked happy and relaxed. We embraced.

"You kept us waiting a bloody long time. What kept you?" said Tom.

Chapter Twenty-Eight

Calviac dated back 1000 years. What had once been a presbytery, next to the church, was now a large hole in the ground, surrounded by ever-increasing brick remains, as the ravages of time and the elements took their toll. With jagged edges, the wall now stood at little over three feet high. One day someone might have the imagination to re-build the dwelling, if only to enjoy the magnificent view.

The garden had revealed a primitive burial ground. No fewer than 15 'sarcophagi' had been found – coffins carved from stone, so heavy that a team of strong men was needed to lift them out of the ground. The promise of hidden treasure was a fine incentive for the effort.

The Resistance, having made the church its HQ, took the responsibility of prizing them open and preserving the contents. There were powdery skeletons that crumbled at first touch, such was their antiquity. Jewellery and what remained of clothing, was carefully preserved inside the church for analysis after the war. One such sarcophagus had just been lifted out of the ground and now rested outside the church door. An ideal resting place for the unfortunate biker now in the boot, saturated in his own blood. His uniform was removed and replaced by a white sheet. A grisly task performed by Frenchmen loyal to the cause. Then he was placed inside it, crushing the skeletal remains of the previous occupant. The heavy lid was put in place and with the help of a trolley, was lowered into the grave from which it had only recently been lifted. The surrounding piles of earth were shovelled back on. No prayers were spoken on completion of the unmarked grave. But Suzanne stood by it for a moment's thought, before placing some wild flowers on the spot. "Je regrette," she said simply, her hands clasped together.

The boot was cleaned up by the same team, before moving the car and bike to the garage of a 'safe' house on the outskirts of the village. At the same time, Tom and I were dropped off at our former 'digs', where the rooms awaited us as we had left them.

We had much to talk about. As we walked across the countryside, there was an element of one-upmanship, when Tom boasted about his night with Monique only to be trumped by mine with Suzanne and she was there in the flesh to prove it! Then remembering poor François in hospital, I added, "Very confidential, please. Not a word." We chuckled at the way we both managed to combine business with pleasure under truly adverse conditions, without really trying.

When we had gone into every detail of our miraculous escapes, Tom asked a significant question:

"So, where do we go from here?"

"You know I have a vendetta."

"To kill Hitler, I know, but how the hell are you going to do it?"

"I have to get back amongst the Germans and find a way."

"I think you're crazy."

"Probably."

"You want me to be crazy with you?"

"Tom, I appreciate the offer. It will be easier for me to mingle, since I speak the language."

"You think you're the only Brit who speaks German?"

"What point are you making?"

"My name is Rosefield... remember? Formerly Rosenfeld."

"And...?"

"Born in Hanover of German Jewish parenthood. My German is impeccable."

The conversation ended there. I thought how incredible that we had been thrown together in this way and now with similar aspirations of killing the monster. Fate seemed to have played us a good hand.

I looked on in amazement. Fearless Tom as I knew him. And I didn't know him at all. We shook hands on being introduced.

"Are you saying that because you speak German, you want to come for the ride?"

"Are you saying you'd like me to?"

"We've done pretty well up to now. Shame to break the partnership."

"Do you think we can do it and stay alive?"

"Does it really matter, as long as we do it?"

"God, after all we've been through, I don't want to die."

"Nor me. But it's a price we may have to pay."

"Not if I have anything to do with the mission," Tom said fearlessly.

We talked at length as to how we might be able to operate.

"We need a contact there. That's for sure."

"There must be scores of agents in Berlin."

"How do we find them?"

"Maybe London. Maybe the Resistance."

"I have an ex-girlfriend in Berlin."

"That's why you want to go?"

"Like hell it is. She ditched me once. She'll do it again... maybe... maybe not. I think the Resistance will be able to set us up. At least give us a safe house, while we get our bearings."

"Agreed." Having Tom as partner gave me confidence. Suddenly the 'mission impossible' appeared less so.

"A lot of work to do from here before we go."

"One thing's for sure," I summed up. "From now on we'll have to get used to talking in German."

"Odious thought."

"Jawohl, mein Kamerad."

We shook hands as we walked. The deal had been done.

Chapter Twenty-Nine

The flight to Tempelhof Airport Berlin was scheduled to leave at midday. By 5 a.m., we were ready to go, dressed up as junior German officers. We felt conspicuous and looked ill at ease. We strutted up and down the narrow aisle of the church and when we crossed, practised the salute. We were passionate about our 'Heil Hitler' for laughs. Raoul directed proceedings. He had worked tirelessly the last 10 days. In touch with London, establishing links with Berlin and negotiating with Ludwig Tortelmann, the friendly cargo manager, lynch pin of the operation. Without him there would be no transit. At 7.05 a.m., there was an urgent call from him. Could he meet Raoul in 30 minutes? They arranged to do so at a local bar. He was a large man with a mop of unruly ginger hair that constantly fell over his eyes. No sooner had his podgy fingers pushed it back, than it fell again. His origin was Franco/German. Of mixed parentage he had the advantage of speaking both languages fluently. As he had lived most of his life in Germany, before marrying a lady from Bordeaux, he was trusted by the Nazis and considered eligible to head the Berlin cargo shuttle. Encouraged by his wife, his allegiance was to the Resistance, although the Germans categorised him as a Grade 1 national to be trusted. As cargo manager, he was responsible for collating cargo, listing it and loading it onto a Junkers transport plane. Then flying with it to Berlin, have it signed in, and return in the same plane with cargo for the occupation forces in Bordeaux. It was a daily shuttle. Ahead of today's trip, he was agitated and perspiring freely, even though the sun had not yet risen.

Raoul ordered coffee. He could see Ludwig was in a state, by the frequency with which he pushed back the hair from his eyes.

"Look, mon ami," he came to the point straight away. "It is too risky. I have not slept a wink all night. My wife will not permit me. When she says 'non', it means 'non'. I am so sorry. Really sorry. Je suis desolé."

"Does she have to know?"

"We have no secrets, she and I. Pas du tout."

"It is very inconvenient, this cancellation at the eleventh hour. All preparations are in place."

"I gave you a price for one man in a crate. That became two men standing. It becomes quite a different proposition, I assure you. We are a cargo flight. Passengers arouse suspicion. What can I tell the pilot? He will ask questions. No... no... it cannot work. Pas possible."

Raoul took out his wallet and counted some notes. He understood the problem of taking two Englishman on board on their feet. "Take the two men in crates and this is yours."

Ludwig pushed his hair back nervously. He was tempted but not yet persuaded.

"The Nazis will kill me if it goes wrong."

"Why should it," Raoul said counting out more notes to put with the original wad. "My men will be in German uniform, speaking perfect German. If challenged, they will be inspecting the cargo before it is loaded. Quite normal, isn't it? Should be simple."

Ludwig took a handkerchief from his pocket to clean up the perspiration.

"And the other end?" The asking of that question showed his weakening.

"At the other end, you choose the right moment to undo the crates, the boys are out and away. Job done, no questions asked. C'est facile, nom ami."

Raoul had nearly got there, but Ludwig was still dithering. More money was put on the table. It was too tempting.

"I suppose in crates it is less risky... I think my wife..."

"Forget the wife. This is a business transaction between you and me. No one else. You will be able to buy her some lovely dresses with the money."

Enough said.

Ludwig pushed back his hair. "Deliver your 'cargo' to me, hanger 14 at 10 a.m. precisely."

"A wise decision," said Raoul releasing the notes on the table.

He had to get back to his 'Germans' and sell them the deal. It would not be easy.

Chapter Thirty

By 0800 hours Tom and I were sitting in the back of the Mercedes, driven by Raoul en route for Merignac airport.

Having originally declined the crate idea out of hand, it now seemed to be our only option. Worse, we had to stay the whole trip.

"Imagine," I said to Tom, "we've got to be stuck in that thing best part of eight hours. Claustrophobic, I call it. How do we breathe for a start?"

Raoul thought it would be a wicker hamper with plenty of air vents.

"I'm sure Ludwig will look after you and see you're as comfortable as possible."

"What if he forgets to let us out?"

"He's a responsible person. He'll want to see you go at the first opportunity."

"Do we bring a book to pass the time," I said.

"The bible; then we can pray," was Tom's reply, fearless as ever."

Sometimes I wished he could be a little less fearless.

"All we have to do is rest our heads on something soft and go to sleep. Easy," he concluded. "Berlin first stop."

After Spitfires and Lancasters, I said it was a bit of a climb-down travelling in a bloody crate on board a Junkers.

Tom persisted. "Your idea. You want to go to Berlin. Take whatever transport is on offer. Beggars can't be choosers."

And so it was agreed, against my better judgement.

There was a jangling of nerves as we approached the airport. Raoul had done a reconnaissance the previous day, so that he knew the approximate location of Hanger 14. He had learnt that there was a barrier leading to the buildings and runways, protected by a single sentry. With his two passengers in uniform, he had planned to bluff his way through. They all carried forged papers, which should work. But the risk was always there, particularly today as there were six sentries on duty, two of whom were junior officers. There might have been an embarrassing dialogue with the 'officers' in the back of the car. There were three cars in front of the Mercedes and two behind. They were checking each vehicle with Germanic thoroughness, as though looking for something specific. Raoul did not consult his passengers. While there was still the opportunity, he swung the car out of line and followed a country lane that circumvented the airport.

They could see the hangars and parked planes in the distance as they drove in a giant circle. Raoul knew the place to pull up. They had to risk the Mercedes blocking the narrow lane; no other vehicle could pass by; they needed to work at speed. Raoul had brought two clippers which he took from the boot. Between the three of them they cut an entrance through the barbed wire. The operation took no more than two minutes.

The hangar is over there," Raoul pointed. "The last one in the row. It will take you fifteen minutes to walk. Ludwig waits for you in front."

He briefly hugged us both, anxious to clear the road quickly.

"Bonne chance, mes amis."

"Merci, merci," we both said and he was gone with a final wave.

I felt very alone and exposed without him.

"Well, now you'll have to make do with me," Tom said. His fearlessness could be irritating at times!

"The walk will make us sleep well on the plane," he joked.

My mouth was too dry to respond as we trudged uphill in the direction of the buildings.

We saw no sign of life as Hangar 14 loomed ahead of us. As instructed, we went round the front. A small reception office was open but unmanned. We passed through it and opened another door that led to a huge hangar, littered with cartons and machinery. Ludwig Tortelmann appeared from nowhere. He must have been behind a carton, lying in wait for us. He was instantly recognisable by the red hair hanging over his eyes. We saluted him.

"Heil Hitler," we cried as rehearsed. He returned the greeting and looked about him furtively to ensure that no one had witnessed the sham.

"Grüss Gott," he said, offering a limp handshake. He was flustered, sweating profusely and looked even more nervous than I felt. If anyone had seen him in such a state, they would have guessed he was up to no good. Looking about him to ensure they were alone he negotiated his way round and over some cartons, then to be confronted by two giant crates that were to be our means of transit. The lids were open. They were like elongated wicker laundry boxes with plenty of in-built ventilation. Beside them there stood a mountain of army uniforms, Greatcoats and other clothing. Ludwig didn't bother to explain that they were for the Eastern Front, where German soldiers were freezing to death.

"Kommen Sie schnell," he said, helping first me, then Tom over the top. The crates already had some clothes in them, obviously to make our stay more comfortable over the long haul. I lay on my back, having arranged a pillow of sorts. I held my army cap in hand, careful not to lose it amongst the loose clothing beneath me. What I had not expected was to be covered with more clothing that was piled on top. I struggled to keep my face and arms free of them and keep the air vents open. By the weight of clothes on top of me, I judged that the crate was filled to the brim, confirmed when I heard the lid being pushed down and fastened with leather straps. I felt desperately enclosed, trapped and over-heated with the weight on top of me. I even wondered whether I could survive the many hours of captivity that lay ahead. I thought of fearless Tom in the crate next to mine. He was probably dozing off by now. It gave me a little confidence that we were in this together.

Next thing, I heard voices close to and felt an attempt to lift the crate on its side.

I nearly stood upright.

"Mensch, das ist schwer," said a voice. "Was kann hier drin sein?" He had to lower it to the ground. None too gently. I could hear him undo the strap to see what might have caused the dead weight. He moved a few of the coats. I braced myself, ready to be uncovered. Then I heard Ludwig's voice, who must have been hovering nearby.

"Nicht aufmachen," he shouted. "Gefährlich," implying there might be toxic fumes or similar. "Für Russland," he explained. "Verflucht kalt für unsere Soldaten, Fritz und Heinrich, kommt hierher, bitte. Schnell, wir brauchen Hilfe."

The immediate danger averted, I felt the power of four men lift the crate onto what I thought might be a trolley, since there was a bumpy movement across the tarmac. The voices told me I was about to be lifted onto the plane, under the supervision of the now heavily perspiring Ludwig Tortelmann. There was so much sweat, that the moisture kept his hair in place for once. I heard the voices shout, "Eins, zwei... drei... und hoch." Not a pleasant feeling to be slung aboard in this manner. Then I felt myself being flung across the floor, to what I assumed would be my final resting place for the flight. There was the feeling of relief that the danger of discovery had momentarily been averted. After 15 minutes, the voices told me that the second crate was being placed beside the first. I wished I could have communicated with Tom. For one hour more, I heard the voices come and go, with the thump of cartons being piled on top. The impact disturbed my air vent as clothing fell on my face. I managed to clear it, on pain of suffocation. There was an interminable wait, before I heard the doors close and the engines started. I knew that the pilot was going through his pre-take-off routine. I heard each of the engines revved up to maximum power before ticking over. How I wished I was in the pilot's seat, doing what I knew so well.

The plane vibrated heavily as the engines were put on full power, then forward thrust as we sped across the runway. The crates must have settled above the wheels since the taxiing process was alarmingly bumpy. And then, we were airborne. The steady hum of the engines restored my tranquillity as we gained height. I knew that we were safely on the way to Berlin.

Tom was right. The only way to pass away the time was to sleep. The weight of the clothing on top of me restricted my movement. I had to stay on my back.

I managed to doze in spite of the stifling temperature. I was happily awoken by the plane losing altitude. Ten minutes later, there was a bumpy touch-down with the screech of brakes as rubber hit tarmac. It felt as though the wheels would come through the fuselage. The plane taxied to the point of disembarkation. I couldn't wait for the moment of release.

We had survived the first leg of our journey. Now the real challenge was about to begin.

Chapter Thirty-One

Ludwig had to manage the unloading process very carefully.

There were four porters humping the cargo from plane to hangar, with the help of a motorised tug. He left the 'human' cargo till last, knowing that the porters would take a fifteen minute break before reloading the plane. The moment they went off was the right one to open the crates. A final furtive glance that the hangar was quite empty, the clothes removed, the straps undone, and Tom and I were free to clamber over the top. Ludwig urged us to move quickly. From long-time prone position in the dark to standing in bright daylight, left us feeling dizzy and disorientated. We were squinting with eyes half-open. We stood quietly for a moment to gather our wits. This did not suit Ludwig at all, who urged us to move.

"Schnell, macht schnell," he ordered. Even in his anxiety, he must have noticed that we looked a total mess. Uniforms crumpled, armbands dislodged, hair dishevelled. From reasonably smart, we now looked 'drunk and disorderly' without a drop having passed our lips. If we were seen in this state by anyone official, we would have been arrested on sight. We looked at each other in horror. Remedial action was imperative, not to mention urgent calls of nature.

"Sind hier Toiletten? Sehr eilig." This was beyond the terms of his contract, Ludwig felt. It was to be 'quick in, quick out'. That was the deal.

He was expecting a senior officer to check the inventory and any delay would jeopardise his position. However, not even Ludwig had the heart to send us out looking the way we did.

Silently he led us, half-crouching, dodging around cartons, to find the toilets. He checked to see they were empty, then ushered us towards the cubicles. "Bitte einschliessen und auf mich warten. Ich komme bald zurück," Ludwig ordered. Then he busied himself with the cartons nearby to monitor the entrance.

A German officer approached the toilet in a rush. His visit was too urgent to salute. "Guten tag, Herr Major." Ludwig knew him well enough, since he always checked the inventory.

"Guter Flug?" he asked Ludwig passing him by.

"Ausgezeichnet, danke, Herr Major."

Mercifully we were still locked in our cubicles and heard him stand at the urinals, rinse his hands and leave. 'Good job he didn't need a cubicle,' I thought, since there were only two of them and that could have been an embarrassing change over.

Rubbing his hands from the cold rinse, Herr Major emerged from the toilet to confront Ludwig waiting patiently by his cartons.

"Ich komme gleich," he said on his way out. "Muss erst einen Kaffee haben. Komm' gleich wieder."

Ludwig knew he had five minutes to get us out. He put his head round the toilet door. The cubicles were still locked. "Wir haben zwei Minuten Zeit," he whispered to the occupants. "Also schnell, schnell," urging greater speed. We emerged looking respectable, far from perfect, but presentable. The creases had been partially removed, but longed for a hot iron. We left the toilet feeling better than we had entered it. No further words with Ludwig. He was too agitated to speak. A flabby, sweaty handshake and we were out of his life. He pointed us in the right direction, hoping we did not come face to face with the Herr Major.

Now we were on German soil, at the very heart of the Nazi hierarchy, Tom and I conversed only in German. Fluent though we both were, being our mother tongue, there were frequent lapses, when we could find no translation to English colloquialisms. We had to take care not to be overheard. We were on our guard. For me, especially, it was a strange feeling, being back in Berlin, where I had spent my youth. That now seemed a long time ago. I had been to Tempelhof airport before as a schoolboy and knew the rough layout.

We headed in the direction of the main terminal, where there was considerable activity. How things had changed in war-torn Germany. Giant black and red swastika flags flew from buildings and flag-poles. The roads were full of military vehicles and personnel. Ambulances and walking wounded were strongly in evidence, being flown back to the Fatherland after action that had left them severely wounded. They were the lucky ones.

We were worried that some benevolent Nazi might pull up and offer us a lift as we were walking towards the main terminal. We were prepared to decline, blaming the fine day and the pleasure of stretching our legs. There was mild panic when a group of military men walked towards us. They turned out to be Luftwaffe personnel, more interested in spending a few days' leave, than investigating why two soldiers should be walking so far away from the terminal. As our paths crossed, there was a 'Heil Hitler' greeting, which we carried out well enough on the lines of our dummy run beforehand.

To our dismay, one vehicle did pull up and offer us a lift. It was driven by a 'Feldwebel'. Should we accept the friendly invitation to join him for the ride? To decline might cause suspicion. We said that we were heading for the 'Tiergarten', which, mercifully, was not on his route. We thanked him very much for the thought and were relieved when he drove away.

Half an hour's walk took us to the terminal. It was buzzing with servicemen of varying rank and uniform. It made us feel nervous as to whether we were properly dressed to be mixing with the elite. We were in captured uniforms, patched up with accessories of dubious authenticity.

A few more salutes were exchanged in our fruitless quest for a Tti. In times of war, these were few and far between. We asked an elderly civilian if he knew of any. He looked as though he might be a driver himself.

"Wo wollen Sie hin?" he asked anxious to help.

"Tiergarten."

"Ich kann vielleicht helfen. Kommen Sie mit."

It seemed quite safe. We followed him across lines of waiting military vehicles including tanks and gun carriers, until we came to a parked Opel with a man sleeping in the driver's seat. He had a thick bandage covering one eye, a neck brace and a wrist in plaster. Our escort knocked on the window, which was lowered for conversation. "Mein Sohn," he said by way of introduction. There followed a lengthy explanation of our need to get to the Tiergarten. "Jawohl, das kann ich machen. Das liegt auf meinem Weg nach Hause." We thanked our new best friend for his introduction and climbed aboard. Normally we wouldn't go near an injured driver with only one working eye. But on this occasion we felt a lot safer with only half the scrutiny.

It was interesting to hear the poor man's story, although related with such graphic detail and hand movement, that his driving ability was further diminished. He told us about Rommel's ill-fated siege at El Alamein, in which his tank headed a pincer movement, foiled by Montgomery's anticipation. They were isolated from the main assault and became easy prey. His tank had been hit, but he managed to escape before it burnt out. He illustrated the force of the explosion with two outstretched hands, leaving the wheel unattended. Worse, he had his one eye on the mirror to check our reaction. For a split second the car strayed dangerously to the wrong side of the road, rectified just in time to avoid a collision. The telling of his tale gave us some uncomfortable moments. We hoped that our sympathy would permit him to give full attention to driving the car without further near misses. We changed the subject as politely as possible, lest he might expect us to match his story with one of our own.

It was fascinating for me to drive through the streets that I had known so well in my youth. Berlin seemed to be up and running despite the rigours of fighting losing battles in Italy and Russia. The Brandenburg Gate stood dominant as ever, controlling queues of military traffic wanting to exit and enter the main thoroughfare. We stood still for at least ten minutes, bumper to bumper. Mercifully our driver did not use the opportunity to give us any further accounts of his last battle or how his injuries had been sustained.

Some of the buildings had been taken out by bombing attacks, which had reduced them to rubble, now boarded up with wooden hoarding.

Shops were sandbagged for protection without window displays. There were bold notices saying, 'Business as usual'. The food shops had queues outside, but limited produce within. As we drove by, I was reminded of Göring's pre-war boast that: 'No enemy plane will ever reach the capital.'

The short journey to the Tiergarten took nearly one hour. It never occurred to our driver to enquire why two grown-up servicemen, destined to fight for their country, should want to visit the zoo. We were pleased he made no such enquiry. When we got there, we offered him some cash, expecting him to decline. It was accepted with thanks on the grounds that petrol was hard to come by and expensive. We wished him a speedy recovery and thanked him for his invaluable services. We were very pleased to leave him without further injury.

I had visited the zoo many times as a child. I could remember the layout, which hadn't changed that much.

I looked at my watch. We had 25 minutes to kill until 5 o'clock. Perfect timing. We watched the monkeys at teatime. Then moved over to the snakes, sliding in and out of the undergrowth. Polar bears standing on two legs, clawing the grill. Tom was a keen fisherman, so he wanted to look around the aquarium, sadly depleted. Anyway there wasn't much time left. We moved to the tiger pad. There were four of them roaming the simulated woodland. They looked friendly enough now.

At the stroke of 5 p.m., a man in a beige mackintosh, collar upturned, lit a cigarette. It was the signal we were looking for. We moved close enough to him to converse. "Wunderbare Tiere," I said the password. "Gefährlich," he replied. I knew we had met up with our contact.

He invited us to follow him, keeping a discreet distance. He walked away slowly and without urgency, enjoying his cigarette.

Chapter Thirty-Two

We felt uncomfortable walking so slowly, but managed to keep our distance. Once outside the zoo, the pace quickened and the rush of pedestrians in and out of the adjacent S-Bahn Station made us feel less conspicuous. They took little notice of us. Our guide looked the part, wearing a green felt Tyrolean hat with a feather in its side.

His Volkswagen was parked in a small cul-de-sac, free of observers. We sat in the back as he pulled away in the direction of Grunewald, familiar terrain where I had grown up.

"Welcome to Berlin," were his first words. "My name is Heinz." Clearly he was an Englishman with a German name. We introduced ourselves.

"How was your trip?"

"Traumatic." We explained how we had been 'sandwiched' between uniforms in a crate.

"But... you made it."

"We appreciate your help."

"Haven't done much yet."

"In anticipation, then."

He allowed himself a brief smile. "Lived in Berlin many years. Wife's German." There was an economy of words in everything he said.

"Is she safe?" I enquired a little worried.

"As houses. Hates the regime. More than I do."

He was taking a circuitous route, I noticed, his eyes constantly on the mirror checking for tails.

He was a very ordinary looking chap. Average height, thin moustache, mousy hair, from what could be seen of it under his hat. Nothing one would expect a spy or special agent to look like. Perhaps why he had survived.

After a series of turns, he parked the car outside a block of flats that I guessed to be of 1920's origin. He took us up to the third floor in a cranky lift, that needed the grill banged twice, before it could be coaxed into motion. He let himself into the small shabby flat that looked well lived in.

"Home," he said simply, leaving us to survey the drab upholstery, armchairs that were elbow-greased, nondescript pictures and threadbare carpets. Rather dim and depressing, but our sanctuary it was to become.

Heinz removed his hat to reveal only a few strands of hair to cover his balding pate.

We introduced ourselves and shook hands. I felt his muscles rippling beneath his shirt.

"You're a sportsman, I can tell." His wrinkled face managed the suggestion of a smile.

"A bit of karate," he said modestly, and changed the subject.

"Drink?" he was a man of few words. We were ravenous and thirsty.

"Thank you. Please."

"Whisky, gin, schnapps?"

"A pint of water would be wonderful to start with."

He produced a carafe of tepid water and two glasses.

"Sorry no ice," he said without explanation. It was quickly emptied, refilled and emptied again.

"Hungry?"

"Very."

"Bread and tomatoes any good?"

"Excellent." He cut some slices of bread and brought them in from the kitchen with some uncut tomatoes. "Sorry no butter."

"That's fine," Tom said, making no reference to the stale bread.

"The wife's shopping. Food coming in hopefully."

We demolished the bread avidly.

"More?"

"Please and water if possible." Our host was not chatty, he preferred to converse in single words rather than sentences. Nonetheless he satisfied our first pangs of thirst and hunger. Never before had stale bread, tomatoes and tepid water tasted so good. We would have had more but the bread ran out.

Our host suggested we might like to discard the uniforms and offered us the run of his wardrobe. He took us to his bedroom, which contained little more than an unmade double bed and hanging space. Some clothes were strewn over a chair. Heinz shuffled them about in a vain attempt to make the room look tidier.

"Sorry about the mess," he said and pointing to the rails, "Help yourselves."

We thanked him. He then led us to the flat's second bedroom. Same size as the first, but furnished even more sparsely with only a bed. It had a musty smell, as though it hadn't been used for a long time.

"Fresh air," Heinz said and opened two windows. "Double bed alright?"

"Fine," we nodded with little other choice. The grand tour of the property concluded with a brief viewing of the communal bathroom. It contained a large, stained tub, wash basin and toilet. Wallpaper was hanging unstuck from the ceiling and various tiles had fallen off. Tom suggested we could tidy up the place, if required.

"It's fine," he declined ungraciously. He left us to get sorted. It was a relief to discard the uniforms. We hung them carefully, suspecting that we might need them at some stage in the future. We found trousers on the rail, which were a little short and check shirts with long sleeves. We were trying on jackets, when the front door was opened. Instinctively, but unnecessarily, we went for DDR pistols. It was the wife returning from her shopping spree. Characteristically, the introduction was monosyllabic. "Peter, Tom. Heidi." We shook hands. She was a bubbly little thing, all 5' 2" of her. Cropped blonde hair with dark roots, an appealing, friendly smile and eyes that had not lost their sparkle in spite of living with her dour, difficult-to-talk-to husband. Making up for his deficiency in that area, she was all charm and chat. She spoke excellent English, with little trace of a German accent. "Look at this," she said showing us a half full carrier bag. "An hour's shopping and this is all I have to show for it. Potatoes, mincemeat, tomatoes and bread." She laughed heartily and showed us the mincemeat. "Probably horsemeat. Can you tell the difference?" We commiserated, saying we had never tried it. "You'll have your chance later. Horsemeat dumplings, boiled potatoes, tomato sauce and with any luck, if I find any left, onions." She thought this hilarious. We joined in her laughter, a little apprehensive of the end product. We discussed the food shortage in general terms.

"No better in England," Tom reassured her. "Ration books and you have to fight for fruit."

"I hear you speak very nice Hochdeutsch," she said.

We explained our background.

"You know your way around, then," she laughed. That led to a general discussion, in which Heinz took no part, on how Germany had changed in the last 10 years, since the coming of Hitler. "Some good things, some bad," she summed up.

We asked her to elaborate just to keep the conversation going.

"Well, you can't deny it, Hitler has built a new Germany. Things were terrible in the early thirties. Unemployment, poverty, a sick and tired nation. And to his credit, he put the nation back to work. He built the autobahns, new towns and buildings, not to mention the Army, with tanks to drive, the Luftwaffe with planes to fly and the Navy with ships to sail the seven seas."

I interrupted, "And the dreaded U-Boats beneath them."

"So from nowhere," she continued, "there was no more unemployment. Everyone was working with money in their pockets to spend. So far, so good."

"And the bad?" Tom got a word in.

"The bad?" she ruminated. "That's there for the world to see. He used his military might to crush his neighbours, viciously... savagely. And now the whole world hates him. He is a monster. Built camps to imprison and kill minority groups. He has no humanity. He is an idiot. The invasion of Russia – did he not take notice of the last war? They don't tell us much about the massacre of the Von Paulus divisions at the gates of Stalingrad. We have to get that information from the BBC."

Her diatribe would have continued endlessly, had not Heinz, who had been silent throughout, interrupted her flow of words with a statement.

"Tom and Peter have come here to kill Hitler."

He spoke casually as if commenting on the weather. There was a stunned silence to this revelation. It was his first reference to our mission.

Heidi was the first to speak. "Oh Mein Gott. I wish you every success. If I can help in any way, let me know. He is a bad man. If he is assassinated, the war will be over." She paused to consider further. "But how will you do it? He is heavily protected. Heinz will find a way," she laughed. "He may not say much but he is very shrewd. He has completed so many projects under the very noses of the Gestapo and the SS. They are everywhere, but Heinz will find a way to beat them. He is brilliant." She gave him a little peck on the cheek, which he returned. "Give us back our Germany of old," she sighed, "so that once again we can be proud of our country. Heinz will help you. He has all the right connections. Anyway, good luck." She picked up the food bag. On the way out she laughed, "I'll start tonight's banquet, and by the way, you boys look very good in his clothes," and in a whisper, "much better than he does."

With that she disappeared into the kitchen, while Heinz invited us to our first discussion. He poured himself a schnapps, a habit borne of many years in Germany.

"You want to try one?"

We thanked him affirmatively. He proposed a toast. "To the success of our project." We all drank to that. Then he said quietly, "How the fuck are we going to do it?"

159

Chapter Thirty-Three

The meeting continued till dinner and beyond.

At 7 o'clock Heidi emerged from the kitchen to lay the table. The meeting adjourned.

"Don't worry about me," she bristled, "I'm too busy with your horsemeat dumplings to listen." She found this hilarious and continued, "Tough as old boots, it is or was, till I beat it into submission," she roared with laughter; Heinz was embarrassed.

"It smells good," Tom said.

"It's my sauce that does it. If bad comes to worst, potatoes with the sauce will be fine." The 'banquet' started with potato soup which was hot, thick and good. The main course was already on plates when it arrived.

"Here comes the cavalry," she continued the joke more for her amusement than anyone else's. If the meatballs had equine content, it was not apparent. The tasty tomato sauce with onions took care of that. However, no one asked for a second helping and the uneaten meatballs were taken back to the kitchen.

"They weren't that bad," Heidi said.

"Too much bad talk," Heinz commented. "If you had said nothing, no one would have noticed."

"Yes, and missed all the fun." She was still chuckling to herself. She reappeared shortly with 'ersatz' coffee, while Heinz filled a pipe and lit up. No courtesy as to whether his guests might object. Heidi had given up complaining on what had become an after-dinner ritual. Hence the musty smell of stale tobacco.

"Cigar?" he offered us to diffuse his guilt. Tom accepted; I declined. Within moments the room was filled with nauseous smoke. Heidi rushed in to open the windows.

"Disgusting habit," she said still smiling. "You men – one day you'll set yourselves on fire. Don't expect me to help you." She attempted to blow the smoke clouds towards the window with her hands. She cleared the table and left the 'boys' sitting round it, enveloped in smoke. A saucer was used as ashtray.

"I'm off to bed with a book and clean air," Heidi informed them. "If any of you want to join me, you're very welcome." We laughed at her final joke. Tom and I rose to thank her for dinner and wished her a pleasant night.

"What a lovely lady your wife is," I said to Heinz. He puffed at his pipe before conceding guarded approval.

"She's fine."

"Has a bit of a hard time with you, I suspect."

"These are hard times for all of us." He was anxious to change the subject.

"Let's get back to business. I've outlined briefly three options of how and where to get the bugger. Your views?"

"I haven't spoken to Tom yet, but the one I like best is Bayreuth."

"I agree," said Tom. "It's a softer target than the others."

"Trouble is, though," Heinz concluded, "we can't be 100% sure he'll be there. Imagine all the preparation and there's no show." He picked up the newspaper cutting and translated:

"A special performance of the 'Ring' cycle by Richard Wagner. Students and parents Free Admission, courtesy of the Führer who may attend."

He repeated and emphasised, "MAY attend."

"Well they can't commit, can they and tell the world where he will be at a specific time," Tom commented.

"Quite so," Heinz agreed. "He hasn't been to Bayreuth since 1940 and people wonder why. He loves his Wagner and the 'RING' in particular. It would be a morale-booster for him to be seen there and a good PR exercise to show the world that he has no worries about the War. My bet is that he will come and choose 'Siegfreid', his known favourite – the symbol of Germanic superiority with which he assimilates."

I had been to Bayreuth and seen the 'Ring'. I was keen to show off my knowledge.

"The whole thing takes over twenty hours," I explained to Tom. "It's a very Germanic thing."

"Twenty hours," echoed Tom, "that's nearly a day and night. You're not going to make me listen to the lot. I'd sooner die."

Cynically Heinz joked, "You may get to do that as well."

They laughed but no one took it seriously.

"It's great music, you may even enjoy it," I reassured him.

"Not for 20 hours I won't."

"Well, if he comes to 'Walküre' or 'Siegfried', it will be slightly less. The first is 'Rheingold' – that breaks you in gently with a modest one-and-a-half hours."

"He won't come to that for sure," Heinz said authoritatively. "That's when you have to get your bearings. Decide when, how and where to do it. Work out your escape route."

"Will you be with us Heinz?"

"No. I'll be waiting with the escape car."

"Are we all agreed then?"

Silence.

"Bayreuth it is?" I said grimly, wishing each other luck. Without consideration, he shouted for Heidi, who, judging by the delay in her arrival, had been fast asleep.

"We have to go to Bayreuth. Early tomorrow. Rheingold is on Tuesday. Must visit before to plan the operation."

"You had to wake me up for that?" she said indignantly.

Tom agreed. "What's the rush?" he said.

"The rush, dear boy, is because we are embarking on a highly complex and dangerous project, which needs considerable planning. Nothing can be left to chance. Do you think we can just arrive? 'Hello Mr Hitler… We've come to kill you.' How do we get in? How do we get out? Where do we stay? What do we wear? What do we shoot him with? Where will he be?"

For the first time in our brief acquaintance he was excited and spoke in joined-up sentences. He was asking more questions.

"How do we obtain tickets to get in? Where do we stay the night before? Where do we park the car? What is our escape route...? The list is endless." He was still asking questions when Heidi, with heavy eyes, half closed, asked whether she might return to bed. She tried to clear the stagnant smoke by waving her hands in front of her. What was left of the cigar was now in the saucer, but the pipe was still smouldering. For once she wasn't smiling.

"I was fast asleep," she moaned. "I'd like to be back there... please!"

"As long as you understand we're going to Bayreuth in the morning. Leave at 6.00 a.m." He was back to his usual word economy.

"Oh nice," she said drowsily. "What's on?"

"Tell you later. Set the alarm for 5.00 a.m."

None the wiser as to why she had been awoken, she left the room to pick up her sleep where she had left it.

Heinz took over in the role of Commanding Officer. "For security one of you boys comes with us, the other stays behind for follow-up if required. Which of you looks the younger, more likely to be a student?" We both pointed at each other, but left Heinz to decide. In years, Tom was the junior and fearless. Heinz judged us well. He was in charge and we trusted him.

He closed the windows, collected some papers he would need for tomorrow's journey and settled for a short and no doubt fitful sleep.

Tom and I did likewise.

Chapter Thirty-Four

Sleeping in a cramped double bed with Tom was not ideal. When Heinz called us, we were already awake, having had more disturbance than sleep. It was a relief to get up. Heidi was subdued, still unaware of the reason for a twice-broken night's sleep. She provided coffee and bread with jam and apologies for 'no butter'.

Heinz looked as though the planning of the project had kept him awake all night. He was silent over breakfast, clearly preoccupied with his 'things-to-do' list. He referred constantly to some papers, which may have indicated the running order of today's action. He made frequent notes as ideas came to him. I was happy he had taken charge; he instilled confidence. Fearless Tom looked as though he hadn't a care in the world. He was looking forward to the ride in the back seat, while I stayed behind. Heidi had helped him look like a student, having found a forage cap, which he wore at a jaunty angle.

"Time we were off," Heinz said. "Maybe we'll be back late or early tomorrow."

"Good luck." I squeezed his hand.

"It's a 600 kilometre round trip and we have lots to do."

"I'll be waiting for you, whenever."

An embrace with Tom, who was cheerful as ever, undaunted by the task that lay ahead. Heidi smiled broadly when I told her that last night's dinner had had no serious repercussions.

"Good," she said, "I'll try again when we're back."

I heard the Volkswagen start up at first attempt. I couldn't do much so early in the day and crept back to bed. I was shocked when I woke close to midday. My plans for the day had been on my mind, since setting foot on German soil. I got myself to look as smart as my borrowed clothes would allow. Then I walked briskly in the direction of the house. It was remarkable that we were so close. I wondered what sort of reception I would get. Would she even remember me? And what would the parents say, avowed Nazis that they were? They would not hesitate to hand me over. As I walked towards the house, a road I knew so well, I wondered whether I was taking an unnecessary risk. When I reached it, I passed by several times, keeping it under surveillance. There was no car in the driveway, nor any sign of life.

I hesitated as cautionary thoughts assailed me. Ever since we parted, I longed to resume the relationship. Tania was still my girl and when the War was over, I intended to reclaim her. Possibly she would have other plans. Was I trying to re-kindle a relationship that had no chance of going anywhere? A German girl with Nazi affiliations. How could I explain my sudden arrival when our two nations were at War? From where had I come? And for what?

If the parents were at home, might I not even jeopardise the project? The more I thought about these factors, the less inclined I felt to ring the doorbell. Rather retain the memory of an adolescent relationship, sabotaged by War.

Maybe a phone call would be more appropriate, a cowardly thought that clinched my decision to walk away. Yes, that would be the thing to do. No meeting now. Phone later. Excellent conclusion, I thought, with some relief as I turned to retrace my steps. Was it fate that the front door opened at that moment and a woman, who must have been at least 8 months pregnant, emerged. She pulled out a pram behind her with a screaming infant in it. She tried a dummy, with no result.

She looked harassed, haggard and unkempt. Dyed blonde hair, pushed on top of her head, that hadn't been washed for weeks, if not months. It made her face look plump, with a trace of double chins on the way. She was shabbily dressed and wore no make-up. A loose-hanging smock struggled to hide her bump. Tania, the once-beautiful girl I had loved to distraction?

As we passed each other on the street, there was a quizzical look on her face, as though she had seen someone she knew, but couldn't remember from where. We turned to look at each other. There was a faint smile of recognition. For only a brief moment it was the Tania of old. I waved as our eyes met. Then she addressed the still-screaming baby and walked on. I did not pursue her.

Back at the flat, I considered the phone call. I still remembered her number. Three times I picked up the receiver and replaced it. With one screaming infant in the pram and another on the way, she was clearly committed elsewhere. It was time to move on and live on the memories of what had been. Maybe after the War, I would look her up as a friend of the past.

I was happy with my decision and felt at peace with the world.

Chapter Thirty-Five

By mid-morning there was no sign of the party coming back. At 2 o'clock I was worried. Relief at 2.30 when the key turned in the lock of the front door. Heidi was first in.

"That was a lot of fun," she exclaimed. "Like going from one end of the world to the other. Exhausting."

"Did you find what you wanted?"

"And more. Coffee anyone?" She was back at work looking after the menfolk, moments later. The coffee was supplemented by 'Streuselkuchen' they had bought en route. Heinz remained silent, engrossed in the increasing volume of papers he had now collated in a portfolio file. Tom did most of the talking.

"My God," he said enthusiastically, "What a place. This opera house in the middle of nowhere on a hill with lovely views, overlooking woods and trees. Look at it." He found a brochure to illustrate. I didn't like to dampen his excited narrative by telling him I knew all about it. So he continued, "Built by this fellow… Wagner himself in 1872. Ran out of money half way through and then got some royal to help him out with funding. Took him four years to finish. Opened with the premiere of the 'Ring'. That's the one we're going to see. It's got to be OK to have survived. Twenty hours of it. Heaven help us. But, I'm quite looking forward to it."

Heinz interrupted.

"You'll be otherwise engaged, we hope."

Tom would not be contained. "An amazing building, seats 2,000. What a size. And our 'friend' Mr Hitler has his own 'royal box'. No wonder he comes all the time."

"Don't forget, he hasn't been since 1940," I said, "so this visit, if it happens will be quite an occasion."

"It will happen," Heinz said, clutching his file. "All this work must not be in vain."

I asked Tom whether he had been inside the building.

"Only the box office while Heidi bought the tickets for her two student sons. Oh yes, I've got bad news – we're not sitting together. Just to make sure you don't wake me up if I should snooze."

Look, gentlemen," Heinz said to bring this light banter to an end, "I need half an hour to collect my thoughts and finalise the timetable. I need to be alone."

Then he sat at table and spread his papers with pad and pen in front of him. Subsequently he connected the contents of his tobacco pouch with pipe and lit it. As the first wave of smoke hit the ceiling, he apologised.

"Sorry. I need smoke swirling up my nostrils to help me think."

Heidi was happy to retire to her bed to grab more sleep. Tom and I had no option but to do likewise.

"Give me just a few minutes to put things in the right order. Then we'll talk."

Two and a half hours later, we re-assembled. Heidi rushed to open the windows to allow the rancid smoke to escape. Luckily the pipe lay at rest in the saucer full of ash. Heidi emptied it, holding her nose.

"Disgusting." She couldn't refrain from her usual abuse.

"More coffee anyone?"

She didn't wait for an answer which she knew would be affirmative. With any luck another slice of Streuselkuchen would release her from dinner chores. While she was out of the room, Heinz gave his papers a final look-over before divulging the contents. We sat in silence. I was pleased that Heidi was allowed to participate in the meeting. Her bubbly personality added a touch of lightness to the proceedings as well as a good eye to assess the plan.

Coffee was poured, cake was consumed.

"Good job I picked up the cake. Fresh out of the oven, it was. A little private bakery. Like old times. Nothing like it in Berlin these days. We'll get some more on the way down."

Heinz rebuked her.

"On the way down, we'll have other things on our mind than your bloody cake."

We all laughed. Heinz tapped the papers on the table to straighten them. It was a sign that he was in the chair and ready to speak.

"I have come to the conclusion that this operation is best conducted by two men in the officers' uniform of the 'Wehrmacht'. It will enable them to carry their pistols openly and in the confusion that will undoubtedly occur, after the killing, they will appear to assist in finding the culprit on their way out, hopefully to freedom."

Tom said, "Good idea Heinz. I agree with you on that one."

"Heidi," Heinz continued, "would you be so kind as to give the uniforms a good press. Our boys have to look a bit smarter for their days at the opera, hopefully in the presence of their Führer. We wouldn't like his last sight of German officers to be anything short of perfection."

I smiled to be reminded of the terrible state they were in, as we climbed out of the crates.

"The boys will travel in what they wear now, with the uniforms neatly on hangers in the boot. Heidi, would you prepare sandwiches please for the journey?"

"But I have no butter."

"Do them without."

"I have nothing to put in them."

"So, dry bread will have to do. As long as we have water."

"I've just had an idea. Meat-ball sandwiches." She laughed at the thought of re-cycling them for the picnic. "They'll be better cold with bread," she concluded.

That problem overcome, Heinz produced a plan of the auditorium, 'borrowed' from the box office.

"This is the scene of the crime," he pointed his pencil. "Royal box at the back, where His Majesty will be seated. Herr Wagner was more than thoughtful when he designed these balconies." He pointed to them either side of the auditorium, close to the royal box and, importantly, at the same level.

"There are three rows of seats in each balcony. Your seats are in the back row to give you most freedom of movement, before, during and above all, after the event. You should be as chatty with your neighbours as you can and explain that your function is 'Sicherheit' (security) for the Führer. You will be sitting alone on opposite balconies. That will confuse the enemy when the shots are fired. They won't immediately know where they've come from and the wonderful acoustics Wagner created will help us."

Mention of a possible shoot-out was a sobering thought. What chance of escape, when 2,000 patrons would be ranged against us.

"Safety in numbers," Heinz reassured us. "Anyway, they'll be too absorbed in the music." Now he went into full details of the attack. He had spared nothing. It was thoroughly comprehensive. He had allocated a precise time for each phase of the operation. It was an impeccable piece of work that gave us comfort.

However, no time or day had been quoted for 'the kill'.

That was for the Almighty to decide. I prayed that he would be with us for the dispatch of the evil man that was our target.

Chapter Thirty-Six

The day of action was soon upon us, after a short and difficult night. Only Tom slept soundly, of which I was made aware by the gentle rhythm of his snoring. I was pleased to push him in the ribs to bring it to an end when it was time to rise. Six a.m., a grey day with the threat of rain from low-lying clouds.

After a frugal breakfast, we gathered our equipment and piled it into the boot of the car with our newly-pressed and cleaned uniforms on top. We thanked Heidi for doing them so well.

"All part of the service, Gentlemen. I am here to feed you and accommodate you but cleaning you up is an optional extra." She could find a way to laugh at everything she said, even first thing in the morning. Heinz was not amused. Two trips to Bayreuth on consecutive days had required petrol on the black market. It cost him a fortune. The gauge showed full, which would take them there, but a refill would be needed to get back. A quick look at the list to check everything was there.

"Last call," said Heinz. "Have we got everything we need?"

Tom and I confirmed positive. From Heidi there was a scream of anguish.

"Oh my God! I've forgotten something. Very important. Give me a minute, please. I'm so sorry," she muttered as she got out of the car. She returned minutes later with a small package. "Couldn't have left it behind, could we?" she said, short of breath.

"What is it, in God's name?"

"Our meatball sandwiches." She roared with laughter. "You'll enjoy them when you're hungry."

"Would have to be ravenous," Heinz said dryly, as he put the car in first gear, to set off on their momentous journey. In confirmation that this was a business trip, he was wearing his green felt Tyrolean hat.

First stop on the way south was a town called Heideland. Heinz retraced the journey of the previous day. After a few turns he pulled up outside a shop on the edge of the shopping area that stood quite alone. It was a red brick building in Bavarian style with roof shutters to match. The shop window had an aura of antiquity about it, displaying a selection of guns dating back to World War 1 and beyond. Every conceivable type of weaponry had been included from ornamental curved revolvers and 'cowboy' pistols to hand guns, rifles, Lugers and double-barrel shotguns.

In a corner of the window, and stuck to it, the owner's credentials – a Licence to trade in such articles and medals awarded in the First World War. Above, the fascia in old German graphics, a slogan that stated: 'SCHIESS MIT SCHUSTER' an invitation to 'Shoot with Schuster'.

"Heidi burst out laughing upon reading it.

"What's so funny?"

"Just reverse the 'e' and 'i'. Look what it spells. 'Scheiss mit Schuster'. Now it says: 'Shit with Schuster'. Surely I'm not the only one that finds it funny."

We raised a polite smile.

Opening the front door triggered a bell that brought the overweight Fritz Schuster trundling down the staircase from the flat above.

"Guten Morgen, Herr Schuster," Heinz greeted him. "As promised I have come with these two young men who will shortly be joining the 'Wehrmacht'. They want to be one step ahead of the Officer Training Course and be proficient in the successful use of the latest firearms."

"Jawohl," he replied, pulling up his trousers trying to disguise the rolls of fat that hung over the belt, "you are very keen. Yes? That is good. Well done, boys. You want to learn about rifles or pistols?"

"Well let's start with pistols. Then perhaps tomorrow we'll come back for rifle training."

"Excellent! The Wehrmacht is using the Mauser HSc. The latest version is an awesome weapon. Doesn't get better for short or medium range."

He went to a cabinet, unlocked it and pulled one out. He handled it with loving care and obvious expertise, before passing it round.

"This is the latest model on the production line now. There will be 250 thousand of them made. My best-seller, for sure."

"How many bullets does it hold?"

"Eight can be fired in quick succession if required."

He demonstrated the chamber with pride, as though it was of his own design.

"Can we observe you load it?"

"With the greatest pleasure."

He went to the cabinet to retrieve a box of bullets and loaded eight of them into the chamber within seconds.

"It's that easy. Would the lads like to try?"

He spilled a few onto the glass counter. First Tom, then I went through the procedure.

"What's this?" I enquired, fingering a switch on the side.

"Ah, good you ask this question. This is an adapter and silencer if you need to shoot with discretion. It will make a minimal noise like a 'phut', that will not be heard."

"And range?"

"It will kill up to 20 metres and more. Obviously, the closer you get, the more certain the result. It is an awesome gun, I tell you, one to be proud of. The Führer has done well to commission it."

Unspoken thoughts were left unsaid. We merely looked at one another.

Heinz felt compelled to answer.

"Very well indeed. I wouldn't like it pointed at me."

The party laughed. "My friend," Heinz continued affably, "you said you had a rifle range at the back?"

"This is so."

"Could the boys test the guns before purchase?"

"With the greatest of pleasure." He took the Mauser with some loose bullets in the palm of his hand and led us outside through the back door. The range was long enough to test rifles and pistols. He placed a cardboard target on a stand. Tom was first to test his skill. With his background as rear gunner in a Lancaster, he was going to be good. He fired the eight bullets with silencer in place in quick succession.

They examined the target. Fritz Schuster couldn't believe what he saw. All the shots had bulls-eyed a large hole in the centre. He went again at 20 metres with the same result.

"I cannot believe this is your first use of the Mauser. Sixteen shots all on target, that is exceptional. I have never seen such a result," he said, now confident that a sale of at least one Mauser would take place.

When it came to my turn, the result was less good. Six separate holes on the target right across it, with two misses.

Heidi, who had witnessed the shoot-out, was not to be denied her bit of fun.

"Can ladies use this gun, and if so, can I have a go?"

Just the question was enough to make her giggle.

"But Heidi," said Heinz, "Mr Schuster is a busy man and bullets cost money."

"Gnädige Frau, I would be honoured to see you shoot and prove you are as good as the boys."

"There you are," she said to Heinz, "he doesn't mind at all."

She laughed out loud, perhaps at the thought again of the reversed 'e' and 'i'.

The chamber was reloaded for her. This promised to be one of the lighter moments of the day. She looked the part as she took careful aim. Unfortunately she closed her eyes at the first shot and blinked at the second. When they examined the card, there were roars of laughter. It was unmarked.

"Mr Schuster has kindly donated the bullets, but at least he will be able to use the card again," said Heinz with more than a tinge of sarcasm.

"I'll be better next time. I'll keep my eyes open," she laughed.

Heinz paid for the two Mausers and a box of bullets. Fritz Schuster was delighted to have made such a good sale so early in the morning.

"I'll take the box to the car," he offered. Heinz told him he could manage without help. He didn't want his vehicle to be identified in the aftermath of any enquiry.

Heidi kept us entertained as we headed southwards.

"I'm going to take up shooting," she declared at one point. "It's such fun."

"Yes, my dear, but if you want to hit a target, it helps if you keep at least one eye open."

"I was nervous. First time."

"I don't think there'll be a second."

"What about on the way home?"

"We're going to Bayreuth to kill Hitler, remember. It's not a joy ride."

"Well, on the way home, it will have been done, won't it?"

"We hope."

Listening to their exchanges in the back seat helped us pass the time. Inevitably, after an hour's motoring, the subject of her sandwiches came up.

"Anyone ravenous yet?"

"Yes, but no thanks all the same."

"What about you in the back?"

"I'll try one," I said more for politeness than desire.

"Me too please," Tom offered in support.

"You'll kill them off before we get there," Heinz smirked.

"Don't be so silly. A decent sandwich never killed anyone."

"With horsemeat inside?"

"I covered it in mustard. You won't even notice," she chuckled.

"I'll risk a half then," he offered.

175

There was silence while they all chewed.

"Tastes like a mustard sandwich," he screamed, mouth still full. "Hot as shit. Water quickly."

Heidi had come prepared.

"Not that bad," I said tentatively, hoping I would not be rewarded with a second helping.

Tom said he enjoyed it and paid that penalty.

"Amazing what you eat when you're hungry," Heinz said, generously handing over his uneaten half.

Heidi was laughing at the transaction. "Improvisation in the kitchen can work wonders."

Tom agreed with her. "The mustard was brilliant."

After a while, Heinz left the E.51 road, found the garage and drove in. I looked at my watch and the timetable. We were within 10 minutes of our ETA. Heinz found the manager. "Ready for me?"

"Jawohl, the Mercedes is waiting." He pointed to an elegant black four-door saloon car.

"Looks nice. A bit better than my old banger."

"It's the latest model. Drive it carefully."

"You can depend on it, my friend."

"I've given you half a tank."

"Put the other half in mine, there's a good chap."

He laughed, "I'll see what I can do."

"I'll pay you well. I must leave with a full tank."

We piled our gear from one boot to the other.

"I see you have uniforms." Heinz could have done without his observation. "The boys go back to camp tomorrow, a 48-hour pass, so quickly gone."

"Well good luck with the war. Would you please sign this receipt for the Mercedes. It's the insurance, accepting full responsibility for the vehicle."

"Certainly." He squiggled an illegible signature.

"You'll give mine a full service, won't you, and change the plugs. They're getting a bit old... like me." They laughed.

"It will all be done by tomorrow, sir, as requested."

176

"I may not be able to collect until late evening."

"That's fine. We're open 24 hours."

"Very good."

We were already on the way as he wished us bon voyage.

We enjoyed the luxury of the borrowed car. Heinz didn't want to be seen in his car anywhere near the Opera House. To request the service was a shrewd move. With the plush seating, smooth engine, silent acceleration, I dosed off. It felt like a few seconds, but was in fact nearly one hour. I checked the time. We were within minutes of our ETA when we pulled up outside 15 Prinz Eugen Allee in the town of Binalach. We were a few miles short of Bayreuth, within walking distance.

Chapter Thirty-Seven

Heinz had arranged two family rooms with a connecting door, allowing communication through the night.

Sleep was not on the agenda.

"You boys can have a cuddle together all night next door," Heidi protested. "I need my beauty sleep."

Heinz ignored her.

"I think we should take a walk over there. Get the feel of the place."

"Good idea. I've some flat shoes."

Heinz drove to within a kilometre of the Opera House, then parked the Mercedes. They could already see it in the distance. The building was typical late-19th century Bavarian ornamentation, with raw brickwork. Large Gothic-style windows surrounded the fascia and an arched roof created the image of a large country house.

However, two pillars either side of the main entrance emphasised that here was the focal point of the building, through which thousands would pass.

We walked around it, taking careful note of the exits and car parks. This was a working inspection to finalise the plan. We stopped to look at the advertising posters. In addition to the Ring, there were performances of Tristan & Isolde, The Flying Dutchman and Parsifal.

"Is it not magnificent?" Heidi said, a little breathlessly.

"Shrine to a genius," Heinz stated, "to make his music immortal."

"Do they only do his operas here?" Heidi asked as they completed the tour.

"The old boy would turn in his grave if he thought anyone else's music was ever to be performed in his Opera House."

"And now, hopefully, we're going to desecrate it," Heidi said.

"If Hitler's going to die, he'd think this was the perfect place to do it in."

"Let's hope he won't be disappointed, then."

Tom had been listening in. He asked a question: "Was Wagner's anti-Semitism violent like Hitler's? I mean, did he kill Jews?"

Heinz knew his history. "He did it all with letters and speeches. He wanted segregation of the Jews. Shut them up in the ghettoes. Keep Germany for real Germans."

"So Hitler practised what Wagner preached. Egged on by the wonderful music."

"An unholy partnership," I said.

"It will be our pleasure to break it up," said Tom.

Chapter Thirty-Eight

Heidi had come well-equipped. A mask for her eyes and ear-plugs. She became immune to the activity between rooms. She was the only one that slept. Not even awoken by the shrill noise of the sirens that wailed the presence of Allied bombers somewhere in the hemisphere above.

Tom and I rushed outside, hoping to catch a glimpse of the Lancasters as they flew over, confident that no bombs would be wasted on the sleepy town of Bindlach. Passing clouds allowed the occasional star to peep through, but there was no moonlight. We looked skywards and listened. We waited in silence. Ever so distant, we heard the quiet drone that we knew so well. The volume increased by the decibel as the Lancasters seemed to be heading in our direction. Either southbound for Munich or looping round to Berlin; we could not tell which.

"We should be up there with them. What the hell are we doing?" Fear gripped me. I was suddenly assailed by doubts on the success of our crazy mission.

"Bit late in the day for second thoughts."

"Just that we've fought our war in the air. Now we're on the ground. It feels wrong."

"Hearing them makes me feel nostalgic."

"Me too. But look at the prize. The scalp of the biggest monster criminal the world has ever known. Kill him and the War's over. It's worth the risk. Surely."

"Do you think we'll make it? Survive to tell the tale?"

"Have to be optimistic, don't we? But if it's my life in exchange for Hitler's, the world's doing alright, I'd say," Tom said philosophically.

I felt reassured.

"Tom, you've been a wonderful friend, and will remain so forever. I couldn't have got this far without you. You've been a tower of strength."

"You too, mate. Thanks for the ride. We'll see it through together. Don't worry."

We shook hands and embraced. The bombers were close to overhead. They could be heard but not seen.

As the noise receded I whispered, "Good luck guys. May you all get back safely. Wish I was with you."

Chapter Thirty-Nine

"I've said it before," Heinz repeated, "and I'll say it again. If Hitler comes to only one opera, it certainly won't be the first one. 'Rheingold' is a scene-setter. Only one-and-a-half hours long. Not worth his while. If he comes at all, it will be for 'Walküre' or 'Siegfried'. They are reputed to be his favourites. I'll put money on it."

"You've told us that a few times, now. We believe you."

"So use today as a 'dummy run'. Go through all the motions. Stick to the timetable, so that for tomorrow's show we'll be word-perfect."

Getting ready, now watching the clock had been a nail-biting business.

Two 'Officers of the Wehrmacht' were pacing the rooms in uneasy anticipation. Heidi felt the tension too, trying to diffuse it with light-hearted banter.

"You both look fabulous. If I were 16 again, I'd have you both."

"What – at the same time?"

"Individually, together, any way you fancy."

Heinz admonished her. "I'm shocked…"

"You could come to the party, too. We'd have fun." They managed to laugh at the suggestion.

Heidi changed the subject. "Your uniforms look smart. A lot better than when you arrived."

"You did a great job. Thanks again." She adjusted Tom's armband. The swastika wasn't straight.

"Got to show your credentials correctly. We don't want to upset Herr Hitler."

We checked our Mausers. Took them from the holsters and counted eight bullets into the chambers, the silencers in the 'go' position. We practised speedy application ready to shoot.

Fritz Schuster would have been shocked to see his beloved guns used for this purpose.

Heinz reminded us, "Don't get carried away."

"Hopefully not on a stretcher anyway," I quipped.

"I meant – don't get carried away and fire eight times. Three on target each will do the job. Then move like greased lightning. Every second counts."

The small talk continued. We had been over the plan too often. But repetition filled in the time. We were finding it difficult to conceal our nerves.

"Look, boys, nothing to be nervous about. Today you're just going to see a lovely opera with beautiful music. Great setting beneath the waters of the Rhine. Sit back and enjoy it. Tomorrow's the day – you may be allowed a little nervous tension then. But not today."

Considering how short he had been when we first met, Heinz was now positively loquacious. I looked at my watch. Eighteen minutes away. That would allow us time to take our seats with the throng of patrons at its heaviest.

"You'll be one-in-a-crowd. Unnoticed." Heinz made light of the magnitude of what lay ahead. "Sit back and enjoy it."

"I can hardly wait."

To kill time, Heinz thought it the right moment to give us a résumé of the Ring... all 20 hours of it.

"You'll have the boys asleep in no time," Heidi commented.

"It's important for them to understand what's going on."

Tom gave me a look of resignation. We barely listened, our thoughts elsewhere, as Heinz expanded on the virtues of the Ring. It sounded like a pantomime, with dwarves, giants and gods all scheming to get their hands on the gold. Then incest, as brother and sister, Siegmund and Sieglinde, fall in love at the start of

Walküre and produce a baby boy – this is Siegfried, who is destined to become the all-conquering hero that Hitler so admired.

He forges the sword that slays a dragon. He is lead by a little bird, to the top of the mountain, where the beautiful 'Valkyrie' Brunhilde, lies sleeping surrounded by a ring of fire. Only the bravest of men can penetrate the flames, awaken her and claim her love. That has to be Siegfried.

I looked at my watch, hoping to hint that there would be no time to hear the conclusion.

It was zero minus two minutes.

"You must tell us how it ends some other time," I said.

"Well, who knows – you might be there to see it, if Hitler doesn't show."

A sobering consolation prize, I thought.

Chapter Forty

Conception of the Heinz-plan had been immaculate. Every phase had been on time carried out to perfection. I congratulated him on the project so far.

"Keep the compliments till he's dead and we're safely away."

"Won't happen today though, you keep telling us…"

"If he's coming to one opera only, it won't be today. Tomorrow or the day after. He doesn't care much for 'Rheingold'.

If Heinz said it was not going to happen today, that was good enough for me. The 'tomorrow' factor defused our anxiety.

Frau Reichmann was lending us her Opel as part of the rent deal that Heinz had negotiated on his previous visit. Heidi was to drive it with Tom, while I was going with Heinz in the Mercedes. We had to arrive separately and never be seen together. We joined the throng of expectant patrons taking their seats. They were mostly young students with parents. There was a smattering of servicemen in uniform which made us less conspicuous. Tom was on the balcony to the right of the royal box and I was on the left. We maintained eye contact from the moment we took our seats. Heinz had urged us to converse with our neighbours and explain our presence as 'Sicherheit' (Security).

I was pretending to read the programme and looked up to see the house filling to capacity.

"Looks like a sell-out." I started the conversation with a nicely dressed lady beside me. She had a young son and daughter sitting the other side of her.

"A wonderful opportunity to bring the children here. A memory they will cherish all their lives." The boy was fidgeting already and yawning. The girl was scribbling on the programme.

"Are they not a little young to be exposed to such a long work?"

"Not at all. It's what their father wishes. He's fighting on the Russian front."

I thought it advisable to change the subject. Otherwise embarrassing questions might be asked.

"What a wonderful house it is," I commented.

"Built by Richard Wagner himself, especially for the premiere of the 'Ring'."

"Amazing, an entrepreneur and genius combined."

"I agree with you."

The invisible orchestra could now be heard tuning up. I wanted to keep the conversation going. I knew the answer, but the question seemed appropriate.

"Surprising. Can't see any sign of the orchestra. Where are they?"

The lady was happy to oblige.

"Ah... this was Richard Wagner's express wish. Keep the orchestra quite hidden under the stage."

"Really. Why's that?"

"He wanted the audience to focus entirely on the stage. No distractions from visible musicians or even the conductor."

"Interesting. You are very knowledgeable."

There was more to come. "And also it makes for better acoustics."

"Is that so," I said, wondering what I could say next. She helped me out.

"You know our Führer is a great Wagner enthusiast." She lowered her voice to a whisper and spoke directly into my ear. "There is a rumour that he may attend the performance."

"How exciting. I do hope so. We would have a really good view of him from here."

This piece of news was received with some concern. I wanted to speak to Heinz, who had categorically said it wouldn't happen today. I could see Tom gesticulating. He had clearly struck up a conversation as well. No chance of any comfort from him. The orchestra stopped tuning. The lights were dimmed in the auditorium. There was activity in the royal box. People taking their seats. My lady friend clutched my arm.

"Mein Gott. The Führer. Look."

I couldn't see him, but her very words took my breath away. How could Heinz get it so wrong? He had given us miniature binoculars. I pulled them from my pocket with trembling hands and trained them on the box. There were six men in it; two either side and one behind. Bodyguards I surmised. Hitler front row centre. It could only be him. A little heavier in the jowl than I imagined. But unmistakable. He removed his cap. The black hair pushed over his forehead, the moustache were all in full view. He wore his familiar camel battle jacket with white shirt and black tie. This was the Führer. Of that there could be no doubt. Suddenly our mission became uncomfortably close. My neighbour nudged me.

"Is he not wonderful? What a bonus to have him here with us."

I was obliged to agree.

Even her young children sat up and took notice. Suddenly, the box was spot-lit. The audience stood to a man and turned to face him in the box.

"Sieg Heil... Sieg Heil... Sieg Heil," they shouted. The Führer stood to return the salute. The crowd cheered ecstatically and broke into chants of "Heil Hitler... Heil Hitler... Heil Hitler." The great man had a smile on his face to acknowledge the reception. It would have been the perfect moment to shoot him down. But with all eyes on him, escape would have been impossible.

Everyone remained standing while the orchestra played the National Anthem. "Deutschland, Deutschland über alles," sung by the devoted audience, sounded magnificent in Wagner's acoustics. More fervent cheers when it was finished. Finally the audience settled to enjoy the opera. The spotlight on the royal box was extinguished, but a dim light remained so that the occupants could still be seen.

The hidden orchestra began the barely audible 'Rhine' motif. The lapping of the waves rose to a crescendo. All manner of negative thoughts took me over as the plot unfolded. How could Heinz get it so wrong...? I wasn't ready for it today... Could I still abort? The enormity of the project stared me in the face as I watched him in the royal box. He was already engrossed in the music; altogether different from the man I held responsible for the death of millions, including the close friends I had lost, whom I had come to avenge. Evil, cowardly thoughts clouded my brain. What I would not give to be at the controls of a Lancaster, pounding the enemy from above. In spite of all the risks, was this not an easier option than now confronted us? Was it fear... fear of the unknown... fear of failure... fear of death, maybe torture? I looked over at Tom, Tom the fearless. I wondered if he had similar thoughts. I smiled to myself... probably not. He was, after all, fearless. To him it was all part of life. We embarked on the project to kill the 'monster' and bring the War to an early end, thereby saving millions of lives. Inspired thoughts brought me to my senses. We had put a plan in place. Now we had to action it. I couldn't let Tom down. I had got myself into this situation and now had to go through with it... live or die. We were here to avenge... I had to play my part. I set aside my negative thoughts. The Rhine maidens were riding the waves below the surface of the river. They had been tricked. The murky waters of the Rhine had lost its treasure. Alberich the scheming dwarf had stolen the gold. Its possession would bring him no good fortune. The music was in crescendo. All eyes were riveted on the stage. This was the moment. I took the torch from my pocket. A single flash to Tom meant 'GO'. Two flashes in return was 'message received'. It came.

I took the Mauser from its holster and started the pre-arranged count to ten. Simultaneously I rose from my corner seat and crouched behind the balcony's back row. The Führer was well within range. I raised the Mauser to the level of my eyes. My right hand was shaking. I steadied it with the left, my finger on the trigger. The music was dramatic at this point. Nobody took any notice of my changed position. The count was nearly complete... 5... 6... 7... I was crouching on my haunches, well concealed, ready to shoot. I could see Tom standing fully upright. Why...? Why...? 8... 9... We both fired at the same time. With the music at crescendo, the silencer's 'phut' could not be heard. I fired my three shots in quick succession. Tom's shots hit the target at the same time. Hitler had no chance. Elation as we saw his body slump forward, blood pouring from the gunshot wounds over his uniform. This was the time to exit... fast. As I moved forward, I noticed Tom standing, still shooting. Maybe he was firing all eight bullets instead of the planned three. I did not wait to find out. I left the auditorium and ran as I had never run before. I covered the corridors and steps at great speed. I could still hear the powerful music. As I hit daylight, it was gone. An eerie silence descended as I found the Opel parked immediately outside, Heidi ready to drive away with me on board. Within seconds she sped around the building, 'blinked' the Mercedes and headed for home.

I was worried. Tom should have been out by now. The two cars driving away simultaneously. I turned to look out of the back window to see if there was any sign of him. Heinz in the Mercedes shared my concern. He gave it another minute. Then he heard shots. These were not from a silenced Mauser. He gave it another minute, but when shocked patrons began to exit the building, he knew he could not delay his departure. "Sorry Tom," he muttered under his breath, "not safe to wait any longer." He looked at the second hand of his watch, prepared to risk another half minute. Leaving him behind meant certain death, if the shots hadn't already killed him. Survival was now at stake. The siren of an approaching ambulance was the decider. The Gestapo could arrive in seconds. With a final look at the exit, time had run out. The tragedy of abandoning Tom weighed heavily upon him. The whole escape plan was now in jeopardy. The shots we heard were conclusive. He had to do it. With a final fruitless look at the exit, he put the car in to gear as ambulances with police escort entered the complex. He got out just in time before the barriers went up.

Heidi had parked the Opel and was awaiting the pick-up inside the Garage. Two agonising minutes seemed like two hours. When the Mercedes arrived, the empty passenger seat told its own story.

I was the first to speak. "What the hell was he doing? Standing straight and firing all his bullets... I can't believe it."

Heinz was driving the Mercedes at high speed to make up for lost time.

"My carefully laid plan in tatters."

"One thing's for sure. We got him. I saw him slump. Three bullets from me. Goodness only know how many from Tom. Blood everywhere."

Heidi pulled a hankie from her bag to wipe away the tears streaming down her face. "Such a lovely boy," she sobbed. For once she had nothing funny to say.

Heinz told us about the shots he had heard.

"Let's hope they killed him outright and didn't take him prisoner," he said.

"So bloody unnecessary, I could see him standing there, firing his eight bullets I don't doubt, and paying a terrible price."

"And maybe killing us all in the process."

Heinz was driving dangerously fast as we hit the E9 motorway. The Mercedes was shuddering under maximum acceleration. It was his way of expressing anger.

We reached the Garage at Heideland, paid the bill and exchanged cars in record time. The petrol gauge showed full.

"Thanks for the petrol," he said.

"Sorry I had to charge double. I did some work on the radiator as well. There's the start of a leak. It's all included in the bill."

Heinz didn't stay to check it. Nor wait for the change as he passed some notes. He was away.

We drove in silence, each of us preoccupied with our tragic thoughts. After a while, Heinz shook his head. "It could have been so great. Hitler dead. Mission accomplished. We live to fight another day."

"Maybe he had a death wish… something he said last night," I recalled.

"Which was?"

"That the world would be a better place if he died and took Hitler with him."

"It didn't have to be a life for a life," Heidi choked into her hankie. "Such a lovely boy. He didn't have to do it."

"But he killed Hitler. It made him happy to think that his bravery might end the War." As an afterthought I added, "You know what we always called him when he was rear gunner in a Lancaster bomber? Fearless Tom. Perhaps on this occasion it would have been better if he had been a little more fearful."

Heinz informed us that we were leaving the E9 to go a roundabout way. "They'll be putting up roadblocks all over the place when they discover he's dead. The whole bloody lot of them will be looking for us."

The detour added two hours to the journey. The delay undoubtedly saved our lives. We could see trouble ahead, a long time before we reached home. The approach road was crawling with SS and Gestapo. There were troop carriers outside the flathouse. This was a major swoop.

Heinz managed to turn the car before a road block would have stopped it.

"How the hell did they know… so bloody quickly…? Maybe Tom…" He didn't finish the sentence.

"If we hadn't made the detour, they'd have caught us at home."

"I'm heading for the airport," Heinz said. "It's our only chance. Can you fly a Junkers?"

Chapter Forty-One

Berlin was under water. One of those days when the heavens suddenly opened and nothing would persuade them to close. Not an intermittent drizzle, but a heavy ceaseless downpour. The streets were awash with serious flooding. Those pedestrians without umbrellas were taking cover, cowering in doorways, arcades, shops, anywhere that had a roof.

The windscreen wipers of the Volkswagen were full on trying in vain to maintain visibility.

"I've got bad news for you," Heinz said.

"Can't get much worse," his wife replied, trying to make light of whatever he had in mind.

"If they're in the flat," Heinz elaborated, "it won't take them long to find our name and from there the make and registration number of our car. We have to abandon it. Take the tram. Simple as that."

"What – in this weather!" Heidi shrieked. "Absolutely out of the question. I've just had a perm. No hat or umbrella. Sorry, cannot be done."

Heinz knew she didn't mean it. "There's a towel in the back. Cover up with that as best you can."

I handed her the towel from the back, the original colour of which was white, now turned grey, close to black. Its use ranged from cleaning oily hands to wiping the car down. She fingered it gingerly.

"That's wonderful, truly wonderful," she quipped, accepting her fate with good grace.

Heinz was already looking for an unobtrusive place to park near a tram-stop. He found one.

"Sorry about this," he said, "we have to stay one step ahead of them to survive."

We collected our belongings and exposed ourselves to the downpour. By the time we reached the temporary cover of the tram-stop, we were saturated. Heidi removed the towel from her head and wrung filthy water from it. Mascara was running down her face.

"This is fun," she said trying to clean up. "They say rainwater is good for the complexion."

The tram soon came. It was virtually empty. The journey was only twenty minutes. Heidi tried to shake the moisture from her hair. We removed our headgear and brushed the water from our clothing.

"So what's the plan?" I whispered.

"First we'll try your cargo plane."

"It may have left by now."

"Maybe the rain will have delayed its departure."

"Could be. Won't be easy." I recalled the reluctance of the cargo manager on the outward journey. The sweaty podgy hands, obese figure, red hair constantly falling over his forehead. "What was his name...? Ludwig, that was it. Ludwig... Can't remember his surname."

"Was he paid?"

"Handsomely."

"Offer him the same for the return trip... more if necessary."

"D'you want me to negotiate with him?"

"You know him. Heidi and I will keep out of sight. Don't mention Tom – he won't notice the difference. And keep Heidi out of it too, until you get him to agree."

"I'll do my best."

"Can you remember which hangar?"

"Think so."

"And you can fly that plane?"

"Should be able to work it out."

"OK then, that's the plan."

"And if it's already left, what then?"

"We'll work it out. Don't be negative."

The rain was still coming down in buckets as we reached the main entrance of Tempelhof Berlin airport. I recalled the 30-minute walk. We looked around in vain for a taxi.

"It's a long walk, I'm afraid."

"Who cares?" said Heidi sportingly. "You can't get wetter than wet."

"Good girl," Heinz said providing her with a rare compliment.

We hadn't walked five minutes, when a lorry pulled up, sending a spray of water over us. It didn't make much difference to our state of saturation. The elderly driver offered us a lift.

"Sehr freundlich. Danke vielmals."

"Zwei können vorne mit mir sitzen. Leider der Dritte muss hinten einsteigen."

Bad news for one of us that would have to ride in the open back. I would need to sit in the front to guide the driver to our hangar and we couldn't put Heidi there. I helped Heinz climb the steps to the open lorry where he had to travel, exposed to the elements.

"It's only a short distance," I consoled him.

He pulled his felt hat further down, lifted the collar of his jacket to cover his neck and crossed his arms to give maximum protection.

"You'll be OK," I told him. I climbed in the front seat next to Heidi. "Scheiss Wetter," I said to the genial driver.

"Regen, besser als Bomben," he replied philosophically.

"Rain is better than bombs, I agree. Wish it would stop soon, though."

It was a straight road and no directions other than 'Stop Here' were required.

Time to slip in a question. "Any news today?" I asked the old man at the wheel.

"Only Russia. Bad as always. Goebbels is speaking to the nation tonight at nine. See what he's got to tell us. Wily little fellow."

I chilled at the thought. Our assassination would go public.

I was peering out of the rain-splattered window looking for familiar landmarks. We passed the 'Stuka' complex, where thousands of the notorious dive bombers were manufactured and I knew we were close.

"If you could stop somewhere here, that would be fine." We thanked him for his courtesy as we climbed down. The downpour had not abated. We were wet, cold and dishevelled. Heinz was worst off. We helped him down from the back. He was shivering and looking desperate, soaked to the skin, water running down his face. Heidi passed him the sodden towel to rub him down. If anybody had seen the three of us looking so bedraggled in the rain, they would have asked questions. No one in their right mind would be out in this weather, let alone riding in the back of an open lorry. I recognised the hangar and remembered the small office that led to the cargo interior. A good place to regroup. If challenged, we were sheltering from the downpour.

I peeped through the connecting door and seeing no one there, crept forward dripping water as I moved from carton to carton. I was trying to get an overview of the vast area without being seen.

Joy when I saw the four porters sitting around playing cards and smoking. They were obviously held over, waiting for the downpour to stop. Even more joyful, the sight of the Junkers that had brought us over, loading doors open, waiting to receive its cargo.

A serious option crossed my mind. Supposing we by-passed Ludwig and walked confidently to the Junkers, closed the doors and took off. With the rain, there was nobody around to stop us… I was tempted to creep back to Heinz and ask his views, when a tap on my shoulder dictated otherwise.

"Was suchen Sie hier?" The voice demanded an explanation as to my presence.

I looked up from my crouched position and came face to face with the mop of red hair and obese body that I remembered so well from our previous flight.

"Ludwig," I said trying to sound genuinely pleased to see him, "I was just looking for you. Remember me?"

If he did, he gave no indication.

"Me and Tom in the crate... you helped us get here? You must remember."

No sign of recognition. I tried again.

"Raoul in Bordeaux. He paid you a lot of money for the return journey, there and back. This is the moment we want to get back."

The talk of money instantly gave him away.

"He paid for the outward journey only. No question of the return."

He knew we wanted to come back. I'm sure he said 'there and back'."

"Out of the question."

"If we paid you the same amount again, would you change your mind?"

"It's too risky. My wife would not permit it."

"But she's not here to ask, is she. It worked last time. Why should it not work again?"

Beads of perspiration appeared on his forehead as I put him under pressure. Podgy fingers pulled a handkerchief from his pocket to wipe them away. He looked harassed.

"If the Nazis found out, they'd shoot me."

"Listen to me. If we don't get away from here now, they will find us and we will all be shot. Your wife wouldn't like that, would she?"

His furrowed brow suggested he was considering his options.

"When will you pay me?" he finally concluded his deliberation.

"Raoul will meet us at the airport," I lied. "I will communicate our time of arrival as soon as I know it."

"I have only one crate free. The other is full." He was talking his way into acceptance.

"How many seats in the plane?"

"Three."

"That's fine then isn't it? The two of us and you will sit." I made no mention of Heidi until the deal was struck.

"Are you sure Raoul will be there to meet us?"

"You know he's 100 per cent reliable. He's not going to run away."

"The pilot is a nice chap. I have known him a long time. I think I can trust him."

A few more problems were ironed out. Finally we shook hands on the deal.

"We'll finish the loading as soon as the rain stops and be off."

"Just one thing. Tom's got a partner he wants to come with us. Can we put her in the crate?" I had to smile at the thought of Heidi in a crate. She'd have a thing or two to say about that.

By then, the deal was too advanced to be aborted. For a moment I thought he was going to ask for more money to ship another passenger, but not even Ludwig could justify a 'pro rata' tariff for his service.

"Just one more thing," I said promising this would be the last favour. "Can you possibly find us some towels to dry ourselves off? We're soaked to the skin."

He was a good soul at heart. He went away and came back moments later with four Army issue khaki towels.

"Hope the Russian front won't miss them," he said.

Chapter Forty-Two

Considering Ludwig was an awkward cuss, I was elated to have struck a deal with him. Guilty, though, that I had offered non-existent terms of payment. If we made it safely, maybe I would find him after the War… maybe.

When I found Heinz and Heidi sitting in a pool of water, they were more interested in towels than hearing about my exploits. They looked around. Nobody in sight. We removed our saturated clothes layer by layer, wrung them out and laid them flat to dry. Even if only for seconds. Our bodies were rubbed dry, before the damp clothing was replaced. Not the sort of clothes change that mother would have recommended; but had she seen the puddles that formed where we stood, she would have agreed that a modicum of comfort had been achieved.

Now fully dressed, save for the felt hat that was too soaked to put on his head, Heinz asked how I had got on. I reported my conversation verbatim. Except I left out the bit about Heidi and the crate while she was in earshot.

"Don't like the sound of him much."

"You don't have to like him to get us out."

"The sort that would sell his mother for a fiver."

"Without the cash incentive, I wouldn't have got the deal."

"Destination Bordeaux? Don't care much for that."

"What you going to do about it?"

"You can fly it can't you?" A sinister implication, I thought.

Heidi interrupted the developing dialogue.

"I'm sorry, I have to pee. Can't wait another second. Is there a loo?"

I put my head around the door and looked in the direction of where I knew the toilets to be. The porters were hovering about, shifting cartons under Ludwig's directions. I couldn't allow her to traverse the hangar. The sight of her could jeopardise the plan.

"Heinz and I will wait under the porch outside. Go here. It's the only option."

"I couldn't."

"No alternative. Wipe it up with the towels," Heinz ordered her. We moved out and left her to it. We couldn't believe that the rain had actually stopped and within a matter of seconds the clouds parted. The sun had the audacity to put in an appearance, trying to make good the havoc that the swirling waters had created. It needed a lot of sunshine to dry the vast puddles that formed on the streets.

"Problem is this," I told Heinz. "There are three seats and a crate. Ludwig doesn't want a woman to be seen on board. Worried about the pilot asking questions."

"Where's the problem?"

"Can you see Heidi stuck in a crate for the flight? That's what Ludwig has in mind."

"I'm sure we can change that."

"How?"

"Let her be loaded onto the plane in the crate. The moment we're airborne, we let her out."

"Ludwig won't like that one bit."

"So what? There's two of us. We may have to dispose of him anyway."

I was allowing Heinz to take control of the situation. He obviously had plans and I was quite happy to play a supporting role.

We went back to find Heidi fully dressed, her hair reasonably dry. The floor was wet but cleaner than it had ever been. The towels lay in a heap, oozing water.

Heinz came out with it in a sentence: "We're going to put you in a crate."

"Don't be ridiculous… you're joking, of course."

"No. Only till we're airborne. Then we let you out."

"Oh, that'll be fun – as long as you don't forget." She even managed to laugh.

"Promise."

"I'll remind him."

"And make sure they handle me gently. I don't want to be dropped or humped about."

"You will be well looked after. I will supervise the loading."

Great sport that she was, she seemed to accept her lot without fear or concern. Even with good humour.

I found a moment to locate Ludwig alone while the four porters were at the plane.

"When do we go?" He looked at my crumpled uniform with dismay, wondering whether he dare introduce me to the pilot as a fellow German officer.

"The loading is nearly done. The pilot and navigator will board shortly. Perhaps you could clean up a bit before I introduce you. It's best you meet him briefly. Nice chap. Just let him know he is carrying two passengers. Then when they're on board, we'll load the crate. That'll be the last thing to go."

I took his advice and walked to the toilet. I emerged looking a little smarter and certainly relieved.

On the way out, I saw Ludwig in conversation with two men in flying jackets. I sauntered over to them, planning to make the meeting short.

"Nice of you to let us come on board," I said, making the salute to which he responded casually. "It's the easiest way to get to Bordeaux."

"Should be a smooth trip, now the bad weather's behind us."

"Yes. I was out in it. Got soaked, as you can see."

"Well, see you on board. Enjoy the flight."

"Thank you."

The crew boarded the plane, the porters were on the final run, as Ludwig indicated he was ready to load the crate. Brief introductions were made.

"Tom you met before," I was uneasy to use his name in vain. "And this is his friend Heidi."

"He might have thought that Tom had aged considerably since the last flight, but was too flustered to take much notice. He merely said that he had expected to see him in uniform. The crate had been lined with clothes. Heidi gave us an amused look as she was lifted into it, but shrieked loudly when stinking uniforms were heaped on top of her. Ludwig ensured that the operation was quick.

She hardly had time to settle before the four porters arrived to load the crate onto their trolley. Ludwig told them to be careful with it.

We avoided the puddles as we followed the trolley to the Junkers and watched as it was loaded into the hold. We took our seats with Ludwig and waited for the crew to complete the take-off procedure. After ten minutes the Junkers raced down the runway, took off and banked sharply to reach a clear blue sky.

Chapter Forty-Three

The three bucket seats had been installed in the tail of the plane, so that, theoretically, the cargo could be kept under surveillance. The cartons were piled on top of one another depriving the occupants of eye-contact with the crew.

Heinz sat between the two of us. Ludwig had the window seat.

Without warning and at an estimated height of 20,000 feet, Heinz manoeuvred his way, partly crawling across cartons and machinery, to reach the crate. He had to move a few cartons to undo the straps that bound the lid in place.

Ludwig, with scant regard to his obesity, clambered over the cartons with surprising agility, to stop him.

"Excuse me," he shouted over the roar of the engines, "you are not permitted to tamper with my cargo once it is on board."

"Excuse me," Heinz replied, " there is a human being in here, that needs to be released."

Ludwig squeezed his portly frame in front of the crate to prevent it from happening.

"I cannot allow it. The cargo is my responsibility and may not be touched by anyone, once loaded," he repeated his warning.

Heinz was in a crouched position by the side of the crate, so close that the mop of sweaty red hair touched him. He stood, stretched his stiffened right hand to his shoulder and unleashed a karate chop to the throat of his adversary, so powerful that the unfortunate Ludwig was felled to the ground with a single blow. He lay sprawled across the crate he was trying to protect, unconscious, hand on throat. Seeing the action, I moved over to help. Together we managed to slide the big man to the ground.

"Sorry about the violence," Heinz said rubbing the side of the hand that had delivered such a lethal blow, "but we had to get rid of him and this is as good a way as any."

His victim lay on the floor with not a sign of life, hair all over his chubby face.

"I've been a karate student all my life. Comes in useful – sometimes."

Together we opened the lid and removed the top layer of clothing.

"Thank God for that," were Heidi's first words as she emerged. "The smell was unbearable. Those uniforms – where do they come from?" Neither of us pointed out that they had probably been removed from dead soldiers.

"So what kept you so long?"

Heinz pointed to the still unconscious body of his victim. "That's what kept us."

Heidi was blinking with the sudden exposure to daylight and patting her hair, trying to restore some sort of order to it. She squinted at the body. "Oh my God. What are you going to do with him now?" she enquired.

"Easy," said Heinz but found to his cost that it was anything but. The lifting of an unconscious 20 stone man and dumping him in a crate proved a formidable task. First we tried to lift him without success. Then we got the legs over the side and levered the torso inch by inch until it could drop over the top. It was hard work and Ludwig rewarded us by opening his eyes. Before he had a chance to speak, we covered him with the uniforms and closed the lid.

Heidi commented, "Hope you don't get the smelly crotch over your face like I did."

She was seen laughing again after her ordeal.

Heinz said to Heidi, "You sit down, keep the seats warm for us." To me he said, "Give me the Mauser. We've got work to do."

"You're not going to kill them are you?"

"You want to land in Bordeaux and be taken by the Nazis?"

"Is there any other way?"

"Tell me about it."

"Your karate chop?"

"Too risky. We're playing with fire here. If they get the upper hand, we could end up back in Berlin. And the Gestapo would not be too friendly. Don't forget we killed Hitler."

"But two innocent men in cold blood is a different matter."

"Don't be squeamish. They probably bombed London, Coventry. Sweet revenge I'd call it. They're Germans, the enemy. They've got to go. Them or us. Choose."

I had heard enough. I had voiced a protest but accepted that he was right and said so.

"More to the point – Are you sure you can fly this thing?"

After Spitfires and Lancasters I didn't think there was anything so different in a miserable Junkers to baffle me.

"If you can fly, I'll navigate." The deal was done. Now the execution.

He checked that the Mauser's chamber still contained five bullets and crept forward stealthily. I followed him, relieved I didn't have to do the shooting this time. It was clinical and swift. At a range of six feet, it was a no-miss target. I noticed that he pointed the pistol downwards. A bullet in the back of the neck was conclusive. First the pilot, then navigator. They slumped forward in their seats, blood cascading from the wounds. Death was instantaneous and painless. We dragged the bodies away from the controls and left them to bleed in the fuselage.

There was no time for sentimentality. We sat in their blood-splattered seats to familiarise ourselves with the procedures. I banked the plane to port and starboard. I climbed and descended. I studied the control panel. Nothing I couldn't handle here. Heinz was busy with the navigational aspects. I wasn't too confident in his ability as navigator. I looked at the fuel gauge with some concern. It was already down to just under half.

"Please Mr Navigator, tell me, where are we going and how many miles is it?"

"Good question," he said, implying that he hadn't given it much thought. Of course, always a move ahead, I knew this wasn't the case.

"Fancy a bit of Spanish sunshine?" he suggested casually. "If so, we can hop over the Pyrenees and with luck find an airstrip at a place called Pamplona." He was studying a map, seemingly to get the information as he spoke.

"How many miles is that?"

"It's only a few miles south of Bordeaux. Shouldn't be a problem."

"I need an exact figure. How many miles further south?"

He fiddled with a two-point compass. "About 150 miles, I'd say, roughly."

"150 miles extra is a long way on half a tank."

"There's a town called Pau that's nearer, but it's France. Jerry would get us, wouldn't he? Don't fancy that much."

"If the options are Pau or the Pyrenees as a landing ground, which would you prefer?"

"Let's see how it goes."

I sighed deeply. We had killed Hitler and lived to tell the tale – so far anyway. That Tom died in the process was immensely sad. It was his fearlessness that had killed him. It needn't have happened. Apart from that, the operation, planned by Heinz, had been a brilliant success.

Lady luck had ridden with us so far. Would she be there for this last hurdle?

Chapter Forty-Four

The most economical route took us west of Bordeaux. The fuel gauge was a fraction of a millimetre from zero. I guessed it would cover up to 100 miles. After that, it would be anybody's guess.

I thought it prudent to gain height to give us a longer glide if necessary. Heinz drafted a 'Mayday' message which we intended to send to Pamplona as soon as we were within Spanish airspace. It read:

'Unscheduled Junkers flight heading for Pamplona seeks permission to land. Political Asylum. Regret casualties on board. Low fuel. SOS.'

We waited too long for the response, which gave us little comfort:

'Regret Pamplona airport not yet built. Suggest San Sebastian airstrip 22 miles north of town near River Bidasoa. Good luck.'

Heinz looked it up on the map. It saved 30 or so miles and was on the coast bordered by the river. We sent the same 'Mayday', but added, "Do you have lighting?" since we were now flying in darkness.

The reply was far from friendly, referring us to the Bilbao airport. Heinz checked it out. "Too far," he concluded. "We'll never make it."

We sent another even more urgent message to San Sebastian, saying that if we couldn't land there, the only other option was the sea.

We couldn't wait for their reply and headed for the Atlantic Ocean. The petrol gauge was hugging zero. Heinz reckoned we were eight minutes away from running out. Luckily the moon was full and its reflection enabled us to pick up the parallel River Bidasoa. The strip must have been close when the Spanish response came through.

"Regret political asylum not practical. For humanitarian reasons OK to land. Lighting switched on."

Although a neutral country, Spain was in heavy unofficial alliance with Germany, cemented by Hitler's military aid before the War. If the Spanish authorities were made aware that we had killed the Führer, our position would become precarious. Even though Spain was regarded a safe haven for escaping POWs, in our case extradition back to Berlin was a possibility we had to consider. Clearly we would seek protection from the British Consulate. We agreed our story must be handled carefully and invented a plausible explanation.

The trouble was Ludwig in the crate. He knew too much. Disclose details of our outward journey to Berlin and we might be associated with Hitler's killing.

Heinz told me he was going to keep Heidi informed of developments. He hardly needed the Mauser in hand for that. When he returned to his seat, I feared the worst, confirmed by a single word, "Sorry."

I was distraught. Ludwig had been friendly on both journeys. Yes, he was a money-grabber but he had befriended me when I most needed it. He had protected us on the outward journey and delivered us safely. His demise sickened me.

I was unable to dwell on the situation with the drama that lay ahead. I was about to land a German plane with three dead bodies aboard on seemingly hostile terrain and now, to my horror, first one engine and then the other spluttered an irrefutable indication that the petrol tanks were empty. I had no alternative but to switch off, hoping and praying that the silently gliding aircraft could hit the airstrip at the right height and speed. The moon allowed us to follow the river. We both peered to the ground, searching for the elusive, promised lighting. I was losing height very gradually, keeping enough altitude in hand for some miles yet.

The moonlight reflected on the river. Without it we'd have been lost. Mile for mile, minute by minute, we glided gently earthwards. We still had enough altitude to keep optimistic. But now there was an additional hazard. Strong, gusty crosswinds from the sea were taking the powerless Junkers off its course. I was battling to hold her steady, when through the hazy moonlight we saw what we were looking for.

The Spaniards had kept their word and illuminated the airstrip. We cheered at the glorious sight. Now it was up to me to get the thing down. It was a perilously narrow runway, pitched between ocean and river. There was no room for error either way. The wind was tossing us around. Too high, we'd overshoot, too low we'd hit the ground prematurely; too far to starboard, the sea, to port, the river. The toughest landing any pilot could ever have to face on no engine power. I braced myself for a tense moment.

Heinz spoke calmly, "About a mile away… down a fraction."

I watched the altitude by the second. The gauge showed 250 feet, as we glided unsteadily through the darkness. The headlights were on, the wheels down. At 150 feet Heinz shouted, "Keep her steady." We were being buffeted badly. "Down a bit." We were at 80 feet. The lights were coming towards us. The ground rushed to meet us. We were lop-sided, not straight at the moment of impact. I managed to get a wheel down on terra firma, more by luck than judgement, and prayed that the other would follow rather than send the plane into cartwheel. Lady Luck was still with us. The plane found its equilibrium. We had landed safely. Even on the ground the winds from the sea blew us about before we came to a halt close to the end of the runway. I leant back in my seat, mentally and physically exhausted. My mouth was dry.

"Phew," I uttered and inhaled deeply. "That was close." I started breathing again.

Heinz congratulated me. "Scary but brilliant." He patted me on the back.

Heidi kissed and embraced me. "I don't ever want to do that again," she exclaimed, looking pale and shaking.

Heinz replied, "I don't think anybody, anywhere will ever have to go through that again. Well done the pilot."

"And the navigator. The tightest thing I've ever known. Another few miles and we'd have been dead."

I sat still in my seat, trying to resume regular breathing.

At that moment my mind raced back to Ginger, who had taught me to fly. I recalled my fear on going solo for the first time, his astonishment, goading me to do better, his smile of approval at my first bumpy landing and our comradeship when we flew Spitfires side by side in the big battle. My closest friend, he was with me at this moment. He would have said, "Not bad for a bloody beginner." How I loved him.

He it was that inspired my revenge to kill Hitler. Now I had done it, he was with me again, saying, "Thanks for that, mate."

It made me feel better.

I took my bearings. We had finished up a good mile from the control tower.

Chapter Forty-Five

We sat stunned in our seats for a good minute, recovering from the tension. It had been my toughest challenge yet. Being out of petrol, we couldn't follow the normal routine of taxiing to the control tower.

Heinz was thinking forward as usual.

"I think we should move Ludwig out of the crate. I wouldn't like them to think that we shot him in cold blood."

We opened the hatch to give a show of light. Heidi was asked to stand outside and report if there was any movement from the tower. It was to keep her away from the grisly task. Getting him out was much easier than putting him in. We opened the lid and tipped the crate, so that the body tumbled out of its own accord, covered in bloodstained uniforms. Poor Ludwig was a terrible sight. The blood still fresh and flowing from the single bullet wound in his temple. I had to look away as we dragged him by the arms as close to the other bodies as the cartons would allow. A trail of blood followed us.

"Sorry Ludwig," I muttered, "you deserved better. One day I'll find your wife and pay her." We picked up the blood-soaked uniforms, threw them in the crate and dumped it at the far end of the hold on top of some cartons.

"It'll take Sherlock Holmes to sort that one out," I said, reflecting on my own journey in the crate. How Ludwig had looked after us, delivered us safely. What poor reward we had offered him. Heinz had been ruthless in his execution. I wished his journey had ended otherwise.

We climbed out of the stricken Junkers and joined Heidi. No point in staying there. We started to walk towards the isolated building. There was no sign of life. Halfway there, a car came to meet us. It contained what we assumed might be a security guard, who had collected a policeman in uniform.

"Buenas noches, amigos," he greeted us. The three of us scrambled into the back seat of the car and were driven away.

We tried to converse with the men in English, French and German with frequent reference to the Consul and British Embassy. Either they didn't understand or didn't want to. Every question we asked brought a torrent of Spanish, from which I picked out a word, 'Mañana', which I knew meant 'tomorrow'.

We arrived at the local police station which was in total darkness, but for a blue light outside that flickered, presumably to attract attention. We were led inside. It was barely large enough to accommodate the three of us, let alone them as well.

Lack of seating made it clear that they seldom had the disturbance of a 'detainee', let alone three. There was a bar dividing the small room, and our policeman lifted a flap to produce chairs from the room behind. He was kind enough to offer us orange juice and packets of biscuits. The first nourishment we had consumed for many hours. He noticed how quickly they went and brought in some more. Then he produced immigration papers and made the action of a moving finger to indicate we had to fill them in. He issued us with pens. Name, address, age, religion and reason for visit.

We heavily underlined 'Political Asylum', with a strong request to see the British Consul at the Embassy. He looked briefly at the papers, gave us a few more 'Mañanas' and invited us to follow him to the small room at the back.

Judging by the bars on the door, this was the local jail. It contained a narrow bed, a wash basin and a filthy, smelling toilet, surrounded by a plastic curtain. Its size was clearly intended for single occupancy.

Our host arranged the blanket and patted the pillow in an attempt to tidy the unmade bed, left in this state by the previous occupant. He collected the chairs from outside and put his hands by the side of his face to indicate that they were for the purpose of sleep. He nodded his head, and with a few more 'Mañanas amigos', and a wave, he was gone. The door slammed shut. We heard the key turn in the lock. We were prisoners.

Heidi was first to speak. "I thought we always stayed at five-star hotels. What's gone wrong this time?" No one felt like laughing except her. She roared, "Hardly the Ritz."

"This time tomorrow, we'll enjoy all the comforts of the Embassy," Heinz promised her.

I wished I could have shared his confidence.

We tried to settle for the night, doubtful if we would find any sleep.

After the day's events and the discomfort of our accommodation, sleep was hard to come by. At one point, Heinz tried to make the tiny bed into a double.

"Haven't been so close in years," Heidi said and had to laugh when he fell to the floor with a thump.

"Sorry dear. Two into one won't go."

"We'll take it in turns," she offered generously.

Heinz and I sat on the hard wooden chairs and used the bed as a foot-rest. Talk was an easier option than sleep.

"I wonder whether Goebbels has told the world yet?"

"If he was going to speak at 9, he must have done."

"I worry about extradition. We have to get out of this hell-hole fast."

"The Consul will do it."

"You sure?"

"The bodies in the plane. Could they hold things up?"

"Nothing much we can do about that now."

"Jerry will try for extradition because of them. They'll claim the plane and its operators."

"They can't do that. Spain's neutral."

"Supposed to be."

"We're British subjects. They can't send us back to certain death."

"I wonder whether the Embassy will come for us?"

"Madrid's about 200 miles away."

"Maybe by taxi?"

"Or put us back on the plane and fly back to Berlin."

"Delightful thought."

Heidi joined in the conversation. "Boys, will you please shut up. I'm trying to sleep."

"Alright for you in the bed."

"Half an hour it's your turn."

"Too much anxiety to sleep."

"We've had a brilliantly successful day. Done what we came to do... Relax."

"Brilliantly successful... Tom?"

"A life for a life... what he wanted."

"Will he be remembered in the history books as the man who helped kill the monster?"

"I think we'll all be. We ended the War early."

"Maybe over by the morning?"

"Nice thought. We'll be on the way home by then."

"The dialogue drifted on till dawn. Maybe we slept a little when Heinz took his turn in the bed. There were embarrassing visits to the toilet, since the plastic curtain was transparent.

"It's alright for you boys. Would you please turn the other way. I have to use it."

She needn't have worried. We had our backs to it.

At 9 o'clock the policeman unlocked the door and offered us more orange juice and biscuits. He was accompanied by his superior, who spoke a little English.

"You sleep good?" were his first words.

"Yes, fine." We didn't want to make an issue of the appalling conditions. Rather concentrate on the solution than the problem.

"The British Consul?"

"I telephone Madrid two times. Number one British Embassy. Number two German Embassy. They must decide. We do not want you here. Please understand protocol."

"What did the British Consul say?"

213

"I did not speak with him. Left message with woman."

"Will you ring again?"

"If he no replies."

"Will you let us speak with him?"

"I will try."

"What did the German one say?"

"They want aeroplane back with crew. They angry about dead people."

"We had to storm the plane to get here. We regret casualties."

"Entiendo."

He rose to go.

"Enjoy your breakfast."

"Look Senor, we can't stay here like this. Human rights. Impossible." Heidi spoke for the first time.

"I do my best Senora."

"Please, we must speak to Consul."

He opened the door, making it clear the meeting was over.

"Perhaps a hotel…?"

No response.

He came back an hour later with the news we wanted to hear.

"Consul come by car. Will be here 1300 hours."

"Thank you Señor. Thank you very much."

"You desire more food?"

"Thank you. Very kind."

He came back with more packets of biscuits and orange drink. Conditions in the small 'cubby-hole' were appalling. We all made use of the toilet and found to our even greater discomfort, that the chain produced only a trickle of water, insufficient to flush. Lavatory paper was non-existent. The air was vile. Our limited rations left us weak, hungry and thirsty. That the Consul was coming made it all bearable.

We were taking minute by minute time checks up to 1300 hours. We tried counting the seconds to help get us there.

"Ten minutes to go," Heidi declared triumphantly, "and we've made it."

"That's 600 seconds. I'll count them out slowly. Give him a chance to be on time."

At 1305, she announced, "The bugger's late."

"Maybe he got lost. We're quite a way out of town."

"Consuls don't get lost. They have professional drivers."

"Give the poor man a chance. He'll come in the end."

"By 1330, there was growing concern. We tried banging the door to get a Spaniard in to ask if we could phone the Consul.

At 1400 hours the cell doors were unlocked. With relief we thought it had to be him. But no, it was a Spaniard with more biscuits and orange. We found he spoke Italian, which we understood. He looked at his watch and shook his head.

"Il consolato Inglese e in ritardo," he stated the obvious. He handed out biscuits and orange drink. "Tutto finito adesso." This was to be our final ration.

"Can't say I'm sorry," Heidi commented. "If I never see another of these biscuits, it'll be too soon." And she laughed at her own joke. No one joined in.

At 1445 there was still no Consul and we were distraught with anxiety. Not helped at all, when at 1500 hours, the cell door was unlocked again and a visitor introduced himself as Gerhardt Hoffman, German Ambassador to Spain. He was immaculately dressed in a Navy double-breasted jacket with spotted bow tie.

He removed his 'pince nez' and pulled the matching handkerchief from his breast pocket holding it to his nose to filter the aroma.

"Good day," he said in perfect English. "I must inform you that we have found three bodies in the stolen Junkers and you will be required by the Reich to answer charges of the murder of German nationals, two of them in the uniform of the Luftwaffe. We therefore exercise our right to request your immediate extradition to the country of origin. I can assure you, there will be a fair trial."

Having said his piece, he blew his nose and replaced the 'hankie' in his breast pocket.

Heinz responded immediately.

"The Geneva Convention states that a neutral country is under no obligation to extradite any person by force against their will."

"My friend," he said smilingly, "Do not talk to me about Geneva. You have murdered three German nationals in cold blood. What does Geneva say about that then?"

"Our two countries are at War and sadly casualties will arise. Your men were killed in the course of an act of War."

Hoffman did not care for our explanation. He snarled his reply as though playing a trump card over a game of poker.

"I have the explicit orders of my superior, The Right Honourable Joachim Von Ribbentrop, our esteemed Foreign Minister, to arrest you and take you back to the Reich."

Were we supposed to cringe at the mention of the two-faced German negotiator, who had forged so many phoney deals?

"The British Consul will not agree."

"Where is he?"

"He will be here shortly."

"His presence is irrelevant. We have made the necessary representation to the highest authority in Spain and have received approval for your extradition. Further, I have to inform you that an aeroplane with spare crew is on its way now with orders from the Führer himself to collect the Junkers together with the murderers who stole it. Our Spanish hosts are in complete agreement, since they, like us, wish to close the file on your illegal immigration."

We all thought he was bluffing. How could the Führer give the order when we knew him to be dead?

Heinz said quietly, "None of this can or will happen until we have spoken to the British Consul." In his continuing absence, it was a weak defence.

"My friend, I regret you have very little time to do so." He looked at his watch.

"In one hour… and three minutes, to be exact, the relief plane will touch down and we will all be there to meet it."

I cursed German efficiency compared to the incompetence of our man, now two hours late.

"We will depart in thirty minutes."

As he turned to take his leave, a twisted smile crossed his face.

"There is plenty more Wagner where you will be going."

He may have waited for a response to this devastating disclosure, but none was forthcoming. As a final shot, he turned to me.

"I advise you to remove your Wehrmacht uniform. The authorities do not much care for imposters." With that he was gone and the cell door locked behind him.

Chapter Forty-Six

"He was a bundle of fun." Heidi broke the ice. No one laughed. "Bluffing left right and centre."

"He wasn't bluffing about Bayreuth," I pointed out.

"Where the hell is the bloody Consul?" We all banged on the door, hoping a Spaniard would appear. There was no response.

At 1530, our man was two and half hours late. The relief plane was close. Our plight was desperate. We sat together to review our options.

"I still believe he was bluffing," Heinz said, "hoping to get a confession."

"How could they have found out so quickly?"

"German efficiency."

"Even when they've as good as lost the War."

"Doesn't help us now. If things get desperate, we'll fight rather than get on the plane. We're dead once on board."

We forged something of a plan. "The three of us should be able to overpower the driver."

"And then?"

"If the Consul won't come to us, we'll have to go to him."

"I'll try a charm offensive with the Spaniards first," Heidi said.

"The funny thing is, they don't give a shit which way it goes. All they want is to get us out."

"When we get back I'm going to report that disgraceful Consul to the Home Office," Heidi declared with feeling. "Twenty minutes to go and that pig will come to collect his prize."

In fact he was ten minutes early. We were released from the cell and ushered into the front of the police station. There were four uniformed policemen to oversee the handover. Outside there were two police cars, dwarfed by an ostentatious Mercedes Benz in which the German ambassador already sat next to his chauffeur. It became apparent that we were to be split. Two of us in the back seat of one police car and the third in the other. We hesitated before getting in, playing for time. Heidi tried the promised charm offensive with the Spaniards. Because they couldn't understand her, she went over to the Mercedes. Herr Hoffman graciously opened the front window to hear what she had to say. She pleaded for more time to await the British Consul. This fell on stony ground. She tried a different tack.

"What a magnificent car you have."

She put her head through the window as far as it would allow, to gaze at the mahogany dashboard.

"Like an aeroplane," she said, "with all those switches and lights. This must be the latest S594 model. What a beauty."

She knew nothing about Mercedes Benz, but saw its title engraved on the panel.

Before the ambassador had the opportunity to rid himself of this persistent woman, she opened the back door to test the leather seating.

"This is so soft and comfortable," she complimented them, taking a seat. "Could I ride with you to the airport?" that would be such a pleasure. Please," she begged.

The ambassador was not a violent man himself, but he had had quite enough of the woman and her rubbish.

"Fritz," he called his chauffeur. "Get rid of her."

She saw him coming and slid towards the other door. He leaned over, trying to grab her, but missed. He went round the back to evict her from the other door. She slid over again. This time, he sat on the seat next to her and none too gently dragged her from the car, throwing her to the ground. She groaned in agony, clutching her thighs. Then closed her eyes as if the jolt had knocked her out.

Heinz and I watched her performance from the side of the road. Seeing her injured, we rushed over to try and revive her. She would not come round.

While the commotion was in progress, a large Ford convertible pulled up, with open roof. Sitting side by side, were two men who looked as though they had come straight off the golf course. Plus fours, embroidered sweater open-necked shirts and soft caps were conclusive.

The smile from Herr Hoffman's face froze as he recognised the opposing Consul and worse, his companion, the Spanish Minister of the Interior.

"Hello, Gerhardt," the British Consul greeted him like a long lost friend. "Good to see you again. Are you well? Now what's this all about?" Not waiting for an answer, he moved on to introduce himself to Heinz and I. Heidi made a dramatic recovery and joined us.

"My name is James Marshal. I'm your Consul and this gentlemen is Mr Juan Sanchez, Spanish Minister of the Interior." We all shook hands.

"What the devil kept you? Another minute and we'd be on the plane back to Berlin."

"Sorry about that, old chap. Anglo-Spanish relations were about to be shattered. We had to finish the 18th, otherwise there'd be hell to pay." The two men smiled at one another.

"However justice prevailed and I let him win. Such is the life of a diplomat."

"We got your message you'd be here at 1300 hours. It's now three hours later."

"So sorry, old chap. We got lost on the way over. That took nearly an hour to sort out. Anyway, here we are."

"I've bitten my nails to the bone," Heidi exclaimed, "and you were out playing golf."

"Ah, that is so. But look who I've brought with me, my partner, Minister of the Interior Mr Sanchez. He is the expert of all matters relating to extradition." He lowered his voice to a whisper. "He'll deal with that arrogant German bastard."

Mr Sanchez spoke for the first time. "I'll do my best."

Herr Hoffman looked at his watch and joined the party.

"We have a plane to meet and cannot afford the time to wait any longer," he stated.

"Look, Gerhardt, old chap, is it right that you plan to take these British subjects to Berlin against their will?"

"It is the wish of Herr Joachim Von Ribbentrop himself, my superior who has ordered it."

"Oh, dear old Joachim, such a nice man. Do give him my best."

"Your British subjects have murdered three German nationals. They have to answer for their crimes."

"Look, old chap," James answered affably. "All's fair in love and war."

"I think we will take our leave now," the German said evasively. "Because we have better things to do than stand and gossip."

"This is not gossip. It's a serious business. You are trying to extradite these three people against their will. I remind you that we are in Spain, a neutral country and the rules say, Gerhardt, that no one can be sent away by force. So to keep the records straight I will officially ask whether these folk wish to go to Berlin."

"Absolutely not," said Heinz.

"No thank you," I said opting for a more polite response.

"You must be joking," said Heidi. "Not in a million years."

The German remained defiant. "They have murdered three German nationals. They must answer for their crimes."

"But in order to escape a totalitarian regime like yours, these are regrettable measures that sometimes must be taken."

"My orders are to fly them to Berlin, by force if necessary."

"Quite out of the questions. Perhaps, Signor Sanchez, you will show my German friend and the Spanish policemen exactly what the Geneva Convention states and it is an agreement to which Herr Hitler himself signed on behalf of the German people."

The Spanish minister retrieved a thick book and turned to a page he had previously identified. He read it to the policemen in their native tongue and translated it into German for the benefit of Herr Hoffman."

"Eine Schweinerei," he muttered under his breath.

James heard him. "Not at all, my friend. It's the way things work in international diplomacy. You should read the convention some time. It's jolly interesting. Now, if you'll excuse us, we must get going."

The Spanish policemen couldn't have cared less who won the diplomatic argument as long as they were relieved of the problem.

The German stormed into his Mercedes and drove away at great speed.

The three of us piled into the back seat of the Ford, delirious to be free and heading for the safe haven of Madrid.

A few miles into the journey, Heinz asked the question that was foremost on our minds. "Has there been any exciting news?"

"Only Russia, where the Hun is in full retreat."

"Nothing about Hitler?"

"Nothing I'm aware of."

"Goebbels was making an unscheduled speech at nine o'clock last night."

Mr Sanchez had read about it in the newspaper. "One moment," he said and rummaged around to find the paper and turn up the inside page that contained a column headed 'Hooligan attack on Hitler'. He translated into English: "Joseph Goebbels spoke to the German people last night informing them that an isolated terrorist group had attempted and failed to assassinate 'our beloved Führer', at Bayreuth during a performance of 'The Ring'. The Führer is safe and well. The German High Command has issued a press release, deploring the death of a distinguished actor, shot dead at Bayreuth, while on active service. The culprits of this evil crime have been apprehended and will be punished in an appropriate manner. Long live the Führer. Heil Hitler."

The reading of the statement left us devastated.

Heinz buried his face in his hands. "I can't believe it." He was close to tears.

I said, "Poor Tom... all in vain."

Heidi, reflecting that their salvation was more important than a failed mission, said, "Bad luck boys. We'll have to try again."

Chapter Forty-Seven

The journey home was exhilarating if not claustrophobic. From Lancasters to submarines is a long way down. Depression at the failure of our mission was over-ridden by the excitement of setting foot on 'Blighty' soil.

Heidi was cheerleader in dispersing the gloom. "Failed mission? Rubbish," she chortled. "Brilliant I'd call it. We're alive to tell the tale. That's what counts."

"I must take full responsibility," Heinz rebuked himself. "I should have checked it. I failed you all, the nation, the world. I built my house on air. No foundations." He raised his hands dramatically.

Heidi consoled him, "You made a brilliant plan, executed to perfection."

"Here here," I agreed in full support.

"Killing an impostor, a poor innocent actor, is not my idea of success."

I reassured him that he had taken all the right decisions, which ultimately saved our lives. "And that," I said, "is a result. Hitler's going to die anyway. A few weeks more or less aren't going to change the world."

The submarine crew was agog when we related a limited edition of our exploits. The Captain complimented us on our audacity and said he was honoured to be taking us home. He showed us the workings of his craft and we each studied the horizon through the periscope. By the time we surfaced near Plymouth, I had leant a good deal about submarine warfare, but concluded that fighting in the air was preferable. When we reached dry land, we were bundled into a Wolseley that took us to bomber command for de-briefing.

Our statement covered nine pages and took over one hour to record.

Our patience was truly tested, when two hours later, we were still in the same office. Tea and sandwiches did little to diffuse our anger. An official in civilian clothes informed us that our immigration papers were being reviewed for verification. We would have to allow officialdom to take its course.

Next thing we heard the stamp of hob-nailed boots coming to a noisy halt outside the office. We were confronted by a sergeant and three military policemen. The immigration officer was with them. He spoke to Heinz and Heidi.

"The Home Office is satisfied that you are British subjects, who have escaped from Nazi Germany through the good offices of the Spanish consulate. You are free to enter the United Kingdom." He turned to me. "It is with regret, sir, that we have to detain you at His Majesty's pleasure, pending further enquiries."

"I don't understand... why?"

"There is no obligation on behalf of the Home Office to state reasons. It is for a tribunal to examine our allegations pending detention."

Heinz exploded on my behalf. "Detention? What the hell are you talking about man? Are you quite crazy? Peter Wolf is an RAF Officer – Spitfire pilot, Lancaster bomber, who has risked his life on our behalf. Got shot down on a big raid. Escaped from Germany... the man's a hero."

"Quite so, sir," said the irritatingly placid officer. "Nonetheless, there are certain elements of the statement that need to be addressed." He turned to me. "By your own admission, sir, you were born in Berlin?"

"That is so."

"You came to England before the war in 1937?"

"I did... to fight the Nazis."

"I believe you spent some time in Berlin recently."

"My statement makes that quite clear."

"What was the purpose of your visit?"

"To kill Hitler."

"A bit hard to swallow, isn't it?"

Heinz interrupted the exchange, "But absolutely true. As a British subject by birth and working for the government in Berlin, I declare herewith that our statement is 100 per cent correct. Peter, I can assure you, is totally dedicated to the destruction of the regime in Germany. Shot down in his Lancaster, he was determined to avenge the death of his service friends. I was with him in Berlin the few days he was there. That is the absolute truth, so help me God."

If the official was impressed, he gave no sign of it. He was not to be denied his moment of glory. He had spotted the potential link between Peter's birthplace and his short stay in Berlin. At least he would impress his superior officer for being astute enough to initiate enquiries. And maybe this would unearth a spy. His mind was made up.

"Sergeant," he called out with an authoritative voice, "detain this man, pending further enquiries."

Heinz said, "This is preposterous. We shall stay with the flying officer until this stupid matter is resolved."

"Sir, with respect," the immigration officer replied, "the building has to be cleared by 5.30, after which, you will be forcefully evicted."

He asserted his authority. "Sergeant, please proceed."

He obeyed instantly. "Squad 'Shun'," he shouted. "Escort suspect to detention cells."

I was not prepared to go quietly, without playing my trump card. "I wish to speak with Air Marshal Sir Arthur Harrison. He is my friend and commanding officer. He will vouch for my integrity."

The immigration officer scratched his head. Doubts assailed him. The Air Marshal was God in the building. If indeed he was a friend of the suspect, his position would become untenable.

Without further thought, he reversed the order. "Stand at ease, Sergeant." To me he said icily, "You will stay under arrest, pending further enquiries." With that, he stormed out of the room, leaving the military policemen to 'stand easy'. One of them pulled a packet of Woodbines from his pocket and offered it round. We declined with thanks, while they all lit up. Within moments the room was filled with smoke. Heidi waved her hands in a vain attempt to disperse it.

"Nice work, Peter. True?"

"'Course it is. Just hope he bloody remembers."

Two hours later, the official returned with the Air Marshal in person. He looked irritated at having been disturbed for such a mundane matter. The sergeant jumped up, hurriedly stamped out his cigarette as did the others. "Squad... Shun," he shouted officially and saluted smartly.

The Air Marshal recognised me at once and shook my hand.

"Read your report, laddie... Well done. Take a 48, then I want you back in action. Put you on the Berlin run – give you another chance to get him."

"Thank you, sir," I said with relief.

Then he turned to the official. "Bloody fool, time waster," he said angrily. "D'you think I've got nothing better to do than rescue my pilots from your bloody stupid, unfounded, uncalled for insinuations?" Then he turned to me. "By the way, laddie, cost of the repair came to £7.17.6."

Chapter Forty-Eight

I decided to surprise my parents. I was not to know that they had received notice, advising next of kin that their son had been shot down in his Lancaster while on active service. Since he was not on any POW list, he must be presumed dead 'killed in action'.

They were at work as usual, when I walked in through the unlocked door. I went to their workroom upstairs. Samples were hanging from the ledge above the door. They fell to the floor as I opened it. For a split second there was total silence, as though they had seen a ghost. Tears of joy, as we came together, kissing, crying, and embracing.

Dad was the first to recover from the shock. "Can't believe it, – my beloved boy, back from the dead."

Mum remained speechless, sobbing. She wouldn't release me. It was an emotional reunion. Eventually we sat down, mother clutching my hands, whilst covering my face with tearful kisses. Dad tried to lighten the mood.

"This calls for celebration. Do we have champagne in the house? Silly question – of course not."

Mum smiled through tears. "Not such a silly question. A client gave me a bottle just last week. Chilled, it won't be, but champagne it certainly is."

Unaccustomed to opening bottles of champagne, the spray caught mother in the face, mingling with her tears. I found a towel to wipe her down.

Dad said, "Dear God, we thank you for delivering our beloved son back to us. The happiest moment of our lives after so much anxiety and sadness. Somehow, I knew there might still be hope.

227

'Presumed dead', but unconfirmed, there was always the chance. If anybody could make it back home, our boy would – and he has… Hallelujah!"

Mother diluted her champagne with tears. She couldn't stop crying.

"You must be hungry and tired. Would you like…?"

"No Dad, I'm fine." We had spent the night at the Savoy Hotel and enjoyed a comprehensive breakfast.

"In that case, you must give us a full account of what happened."

"How long have you got?"

"We want to hear every detail."

I took a deep breath, sipped my champagne and began at the beginning. Even a shortened resumé took two hours to relate.

Mum said, "Like a fairy-tale, you're back home safe."

Dad said, "With all the twists and turns, it's an unbelievable story. You should write a book with all your adventures and narrow escapes."

"Wish I could. People wouldn't believe it, would they?"

After dinner it was pleasant to be back in my room, lying on my old bed. As I drifted to sleep, I planned the following day. Top of my agenda, was the phone call I had been planning for weeks.

It was 11 a.m. I waited until I had the breakfast room to myself. Then nervously dialled the number.

"Hello, is that Suzy?" I knew it was.

"Yes. Who's that?"

"It's Peter." She was too well-mannered to ask Peter who? I needed to give more information.

"Ginger's friend. You remember me?"

"Of course I do. How are you?"

"Fine. Sorry I haven't been in touch, a bit busy."

"I understand. We all are with this terrible War… I'm sorry Bunny's out. Shall I tell her you called?"

"No, not really…" Then came the hardest sentence of the call: "It's you I want to talk to."

There was a pause in the conversation. I hoped she wouldn't say 'What about?'

I quickly asked a question, "Am I too late for Ophelia?"

"I'm afraid you are. I'm resting at the moment."

"In that case will you join me for lunch tomorrow?"

"Thank you. That would be lovely."

I knew she was the girl I wanted to spend the rest of my life with, the moment I saw her. I kissed her on both cheeks. She reciprocated.

"Ginger said I could look all I wanted, but mustn't touch."

"Poor Ginger. He was lovely."

"Ginger is with me every moment of every day. I see him. I hear him and d'you know what he's saying to me right now?"

"I can't imagine," she said with a sweet smile.

"He's saying, Now that I've gone, there's no one in the wide world better to look after you than Peter, my dearest friend."

"Well that's a kindly thought. Thank you Ginger."

"True or false," I challenged her.

"You're flying Lancasters. I couldn't bear to be a war widow again. You've no idea of what I went through."

"Shall I tell you how I reacted to Ginger's death. I was obsessed with revenge. I set out to 'Kill Hitler'. That's what I've been doing since you last saw me."

"And did you?" she said with a hint of disbelief.

For the second time in as many days, I told my story in explicit detail. She was stunned.

"It has to be a book," she exclaimed, spellbound on hearing the story to its end.

"I can't write a book. Wouldn't know where to start."

"But I can. We'll do it together. I'll write... you edit." Her eyes were sparkling with the excitement of the project. Far preferable to 'Resting'.

"Tell you what," she went on, "I'll write the introduction tonight... we'll take it from there."

We talked about the project until past 7 o'clock.

The maître d' had been hovering around our table for 30 minutes. Finally he approached the luncheon diners. "I'm so sorry Monsieur, Madame, the table is reserved for dinner tonight. Our guests will be arriving soon. I much regret we need to prepare the table."

As we rose to leave, she concluded, "It's an amazing story. I hope I can do it justice."

"It'll be fun working together. I'll get to know you better."

"Ad nauseam."

"Nonsense. I'll enjoy every minute."

"No sleep tonight. I'll write the dedication. We must meet tomorrow to plan the chapters. I'm so excited."

"Me too," more at the prospect of working with her so closely, than the end product. I was reluctant to let her go. We agreed to meet again the next day, same place same time.

She arrived, looking quite different. This was her 'work-in-progress' look. Hair in a chignon with loose strands hanging casually over her cheeks, a smock type sweater dress, slacks and flat shoes. She carried a thick pad, which she placed on the table to take notes. If there had been little sleep that night, she showed no sign of it.

Before we ordered, she insisted on reading me the dedication she had written overnight. In a soft sad voice with beautiful intonation, it was the first evidence of her writing ability. When she finished – it was only a few lines – I asked her to read it again.

"That's perfect," I said, and added with a smile, "couldn't have done it better myself."

The maître d' hovered around, poised to take our order. We were too excited at that moment to think about food and ordered a carafe of house wine to start with.

"We need to go through the story and allocate chapters with content."

"Sounds a good idea," I said, thinking it would be much more fun to kiss her, than go through it all again. No chance of that as she quizzed me on my early life in Berlin. She was taking notes feverishly. We got to chapter three, when the maître d' approached us again.

"I apologise, Monsieur, Madame, but the kitchen will close in five minutes, if you wish to order."

We chose corned beef fritters and continued with our work. We outlined chapter four as we ate. We were so engrossed in sketching the storyline, that we lost track of time. At 7 o'clock, the maître d' wanted his table back for the evening session. By then it was littered with sheets of script, notes and anecdotes.

"We need more time," she pleaded. "Could we stay for dinner?"

He went away to study his bookings. "Yes, that will be in order. I can fit you in, I believe."

We were alone in the restaurant at 7.30 and it didn't look as though 'fitting us in' had been too much of a problem. When we left at midnight, only two other tables were occupied. I took her home and kissed her on the doorstep, a modest peck on the cheek, to which she responded favourably.

"Must go," I said hastily, not wanting to run into Bunny, who was unaware of the project. For seven days we sat together at the same table, right through the afternoon and evening. The maître d' was by now accustomed to our two-meal routine and not a little dismayed when we persisted in ordering only sandwiches for one of them.

"We are a restaurant, Monsieur, Madame," he said spitefully, "not a sandwich bar."

Nonetheless, in view of our steady custom, he prevailed.

On the seventh night, Suzy's notebook had reached chapter 48. It was an exhausting and emotional experience for us both. Suzy had filled six thick pads with her data. The chapter outlines had been completed. Now it was up to her to put flesh on the bones.

My ten days' leave came to an end. I was due back on active service. Suzy must have noticed the changing pattern of my day. But no word on the matter was spoken. We met each day at about 2 p.m. and to get back in time for briefing, I had to leave by 3.30. I never wore uniform and made no mention of my nightly bombing raids. But of course, I knew that she knew.

She would read to me the pages that she had written. I made a few amendments, but never failed to congratulate her on her style and understanding. The Spitfire and Lancaster chapters needed my input, but the human elements of the story were recorded in a simple and moving way.

The chapter covering Ginger's death had us both in tears. We consoled each other by holding hands. I thought it the perfect moment to kiss her. She did not object.

By chapter ten we were lovers. We enjoyed intimate moments on the heath and at her flat when Bunny was out. It was total mutual fulfilment. We were in love.

By chapter 18 we spoke of marriage.

At chapter 34 she broke the news. It was a shame baby couldn't wait for the ceremony.

But book-wise it was perfect timing.

Well into her eighth month she read me the penultimate chapter with a flourish.

"Darling, you've done a brilliant job. I am so impressed."

"Now what to do with it."

"Send it to a publisher of course. Someone will snap it up."

"Will they believe it or think it's fiction."

"What they think is up to them. Do we care?"

"What do we call it?"

"'KILL HITLER' by Suzy Wolf. Sounds good. Very good."

"A bit premature, isn't it?"

"We'll be married by then."

"Is that a proposal I hear?"

"No, it's an order."

I got down on one knee. "Darling, I love you passionately with all my heart. Will you marry me?"

"Yes and I love you too. Can I have Bunny as my maid of honour?"

We both laughed so much. It was the moment that the contractions started.

"Darling, I think baby wants to join us soon."

The little MG had never been driven faster. We arrived at the hospital in record time. I paced the waiting room hour after hour. Every time a nurse appeared, I asked for news.

"Don't worry, sir. Everything is going just fine. Baby will come when it's good and ready. Might be tomorrow, if not tonight."

I was due for briefing on tonight's raid in two hours. Clearly baby was not going to arrive in time.

I phoned my CO to ask for compassionate leave to stay the night.

"The Air Marshal wants 1000 bombers for the Berlin run tonight. 999 won't do."

"I know the Air Marshal very well. He'd understand my predicament."

"Well just this once," he said showing his kindly streak, "but don't make a habit of it."

"Thank you, sir," I said gratefully and prepared for an all-night vigil.

Our baby boy arrived at 10.15 the next morning. Mother and baby were fine. Father less so.

We held our beautiful baby tightly in our arms and kissed him.

We stroked his fine down of ash blond hair.

"Shall we call him Ginger?"

IN MEMORIAM

*7th September 2000, it was the day Ginger died 60 years ago.
I wanted to get as close to him as I could.*

*I begged my family to get me out of hospital and take me to the old
aerodrome at Duxford.*

*Suzy had painkillers with her in case the stomach cramps
paralysed me.*

She held my hand all the way.

*My two sons pushed the wheelchair over stony ground on a bumpy
ride.*

*My four grandchildren played hide-and-seek, unaware of the
solemnity of the occasion.*

The grass was overgrown. It was hard to be precise.

*I guided them near to the spot where I believe his Spitfire had
crashed.*

I felt close to death.

*I was longing to tell him how I had landed the Junkers successfully
in conditions of extreme peril.*